TIME
MANAGEMENT
FOR
UnTmAnagEablE
PEOPLE

ANN McGEE-COOPER

WITH

DUANE TRAMMELL

BANTAM BOOKS
NEW YORK • TORONTO • LONDON • SYDNEY • AUCKLAND

TIME MANAGEMENT FOR UNMANAGEABLE PEOPLE
A Bantam Book / September 1994

PUBLISHING HISTORY
Originally Published by Bowen & Rogers 1993

Library of Congress Cataloging-in-Publication Data

McGee-Cooper, Ann.
   Time management for unmanageable people / Ann McGee-Cooper with
Duane Trammell.
      p.   cm.
   Includes bibliographical references and index.
   ISBN 0-553-37071-5
   1. Time management.   I. Trammell, Duane.   II. Title.
HD69.T54M4   1994
650.1—dc20   93-47683
                                                                CIP

Published simultaneously in the United States and Canada

Bantam Books are published by Bantam Books, a division of Bantam
Doubleday Dell Publishing Group, Inc. Its trademark, consisting of the
words "Bantam Books" and the portrayal of a rooster, is Registered in
U.S. Patent and Trademark Office and in other countries. Marca
Registrada. Bantam Books, 1540 Broadway, New York, New York 10036.

PRINTED IN THE UNITED STATES OF AMERICA
20 19 18 17 16 15 14 13

QUANTITY SALES

Most Bantam books are available at special quantity discounts when purchased in bulk by corporations, organizations or groups. Special imprints, messages and excerpts can be produced to meet your needs. For more information, write to: Bantam Books, 1540 Broadway, New York, NY 10036. Attention: Director, Diversified Sales.

Please specify how you intend to use the books (e.g., promotion, resale, etc.).

INDIVIDUAL SALES

Are there any Bantam books you want but cannot find in your local stores? If so, you can order them directly from us. You can get any Bantam book currently in print. For a complete, up-to-date listing of our books, and information on how to order, write to: Bantam Books, 1540 Broadway, New York, NY 10036. Attention: Customer Service.

WHAT THE EXPERTS ARE SAYING ABOUT
TIME MANAGEMENT FOR UNMANAGEABLE PEOPLE

"Communicates the absolute requisite for balance in our lives. With compelling logic, Ann gives us permission and tools to know when and how to seek perfection. She also reminds us to rethink our perception of time and just how carefully we must use it.**"**

—Leslie G. McCraw
Chairman and CEO, Fluor Corporation

"Outstanding book! Immense value—and fun! Gives us a new way to look at the familiar and see things we never saw before.**"**

—Jim Young
**Assistant to the Chairman
Electronic Data Systems Corp.**

"A playful yet practical approach. Shows how to have the time of your life . . . and a life filled with good times.**"**

—Dr. Joel Goodman, **Director**
**The Humor Project, Inc.
Saratoga Springs, New York**

"Inspiring and insightful—shows you how to conjure up unknown time reserves. Full of organizing skills, ways to increase quality and balance your life—and sheer enjoyment!**"**

—Dr. Lothar J. Seiwert
**Professor of Personal Management
Author of** *Time Is Money: Save It*

"Terrific! Helps me think about important issues in creative, fun, and useful ways.**"**

—Jack Lowe
CEO, TDIndustries

"An enjoyable and practical guide for organizing the chronically disorganized. Insightful and valuable— helps us appreciate the benefits of a different and more creative approach to accomplishing our work.**"**

—Paul J. Varello
Chairman/CEO, American Ref-Fuel Company

"A great how-to book for unique, creative people.**"**

—Peter Van Nort
President, H. B. Zachry Company

"'Time Management for Unmanageable People' offers a sane and entertaining look at the subject we all bemoan: time and the lack of it. This book acknowledges the differences of humans and their multiple approaches to time and does so in a people-friendly manner.**"**

—Joline Godfrey
Cofounder of An Income of Her Own
Author of *Our Wildest Dreams:*
Women Entrepreneurs Making Money,
Having Fun, Doing Good

"The perfect book for these times. Lively, creative, and full of extraordinarily practical ideas. In an inspiring way, it helps us decide how to allocate our time and, in doing so, increase our personal credibility.**"**

—Jim Kouzes, President
Tom Peters Group/Learning Systems
Coauthor of *The Leadership*
Challenge and *Credibility*

Dedication

TO YOU

the wonderfully creative

and somewhat chaotic people

who work from a collection

of daily to-do lists

whose length and detail rival

the New York City phone book,

whose files disappear amid

the sea of confusion

created by a work style

that moves in six directions at once

and is predictably unpredictable,

whose best intentions at follow-through

get lost as you are struck

by a fresh inspiration

or bored by yesterday's unfinished agenda.

May you be entertained,

freed from guilt,

and inspired

by a fresh approach to

balance in your life.

Contents

PART

MENTAL SOFTWARE THAT UNCOVERS HIDDEN TIME

F o r e w o r d

by Larry Dossey, M.D.

I've learned some important lessons in life from Chinese fortune cookies. One of the most painful came one night around midnight as I hurriedly dined alone in my favorite Chinese restaurant. As a young physician, I had finished a hectic day at the hospital that involved several very sick and dying patients. I had not stopped to eat all day and was famished, in addition to being completely exhausted. Even though it was late and the restaurant was closing, I knew that the owner would allow me to dine quickly while the staff cleaned up. After gulping my meal and getting ready to hurry home to collapse in bed before beginning another frantic day, I was presented with the fortune cookie. It said:

"WHEN NOTHING IS PRESSING, PUTTER AROUND WITH THIS OR THAT."

Larry Dossey, M.D., is a physician of internal medicine and the author of five books: *Meaning & Medicine; Recovering the Soul; Beyond Illness; Space, Time & Medicine;* and *Healing Words: The Power of Prayer and the Practice of Medicine.*

I was stunned. This fragile, inanimate fortune cookie had looked inside my head, read my mind, and given me the lesson I most needed at that moment: Slow down!

What is time, this entity that we want to "manage"? Nobel Prize–winning physicist Richard Feynman once said that physicists work with time every day. But don't ask what it is, he warned, because it is simply "too difficult." Whatever time is, one thing seems certain: it is not the external, objective, flowing substance once envisioned by classical scientists. In fact, *never in the history of science has an experiment shown that time flows.*

In spite of this, we grow up believing that time is a "thing" that is external and objective, that flows from birth to death, and that we sooner or later will run out of. This is one of the most pernicious and damaging ideas we ever develop. It can, in fact, be fatal.

One of the most important medical insights of our century is that one's awareness of time is translated into the body. Pathological time awareness and psychological stress are so inextricably linked that they are in some sense synonymous. Feelings of time pressure are not merely aggravations that simply float somewhere in the mind, lodged safely above the clavicles, isolated from the rest of the body. Our time sense enters our entire body as profoundly as blood and oxygen—and it can kill or preserve us, serve or slay us.

I learned about "hurry sickness," which Ann McGee-Cooper and Duane Trammell discuss in this book, firsthand. Certain illnesses crop up frequently in the lives of persons possessed by a harassing sense of time pressure. From my early teens I suffered from incapacitating migraine headaches that were related to self-imposed stresses and deadlines of all sorts. This illness nearly ended my career as a doctor, but it was almost totally eliminated as I eventually learned a different way of *being,* a new way of regarding time, through biofeedback training.

Just as we are learning more about hurry sickness, we are learning more about time therapies as well. That is why Ann McGee-Cooper and Duane Trammell are really "time therapists," and why *Time Management for Unmanageable People* can literally save lives.

"Millions long for immortality who do not know what to do with themselves on a rainy Sunday afternoon," Susan Ertz once said, implying that unless we know how to dwell fully in the present, the happiness and peace we seek in our lives will continually elude us. Thus *Time Management for Unmanageable People* goes beyond conventional concepts of time management, efficiency, the bottom line, and even hurry sickness, as important as these issues are. This book is a gentle nudge to discover who we really are and how we fit spiritually into this wondrous world.

I sometimes think that books on time management are best written by women and particularly by mothers, such as Ann McGee-Cooper. Perhaps there is something in the monthly periodic cycle of a woman's body or the cycle of a mother's gestation that cannot be hurried and that makes possible an understanding of time and patience that, in contrast, is acquired by men only with great difficulty. But these are speculations. What is not speculative is that Ann McGee-Cooper is a growing legend in her field. Her teaching methods and writing style embody a fluid grace that emerges from her own gentleness and personal understanding, and she attracts talented people around her like her award-winning colleague, Duane Trammell. They are wise guides who together have written a very wise book, which it is my distinct honor to recommend.

Introduction

IF IT'S SO GREAT, WHY DOESN'T IT WORK FOR ALL OF US?

I t would be hard to find a person who has not read a book or article on getting organized, or who has not listened to a tape, been to a seminar, or, at the very least, thought about time management. Everyone is interested in learning how to use his or her time more wisely.

About twenty years ago, I was asked to teach a course on time management to a business group. If anyone needed it, I did, so I thought it would be a great opportunity for me to learn how to get my own life together while I was teaching the principles to the corporate group. It was fun getting all the course materials together, and it made such good sense! Plan, prioritize, schedule, do it ... even *I* could memorize those simple steps.

I discovered a very valuable lesson from teaching those first time management courses. The system seemed to work beautifully for half of the class, but in less than a week, the other half of the class (myself included!) again had dozens of projects in motion simultaneously, phone messages taped to every surface, and files piled all over the room. But I noticed something else, too. We managed to get as much done as our linear counterparts and sometimes we did even more.

As I continued to visit the offices of executives at every level in organizations and confessed my own sins of a desk stacked high with files in motion and yesterday's half-eaten lunch container of chop suey, they began to show me their own secret pockets of "disorganization." Not only was I not alone in my sea of stuff, I was in very respectable company. Somehow, these highly admired individuals had made it to the top of their fields without meticulously writing down all of the day's activities in a spiral-bound diary or work record or following all the other classic rules for getting organized.

Over the course of the next few years, I discovered that there was more to it than just giving us right-brainers permission to have a messy desk. It really wasn't a messy desk at all—it was a different way of organizing. There was a system to those piles of stuff. The stacks by the phone were things I was waiting for people to call me back on. The stacks on the top of the desk were projects in motion I needed to remind myself about

Brain Engineering

Since 1980, we at Ann McGee-Cooper and Associates, Inc., have been tracking concepts, strategies, and new learning across a broad range of fields relating to the brain, human potential, learning, and performance. By studying advances in the sciences, philosophy, business, education, environmental issues, and health, we seek to synthesize common findings and identify patterns for practical applications. We call this process Brain Engineering.

Rapid change in society creates both problems to solve and opportunities for advancement. By partnering with clients, we create together a range of new strategies for dealing with leadership challenges, newly organized business teams, continuous performance improvements, and burnout and stress in the workplace, as well as for developing innovative thinking and an appreciation of diversity. Brain Engineering helps us see answers when they are hard to find.

so that solutions could incubate. The files above the wastepaper basket were things I was 80 percent sure I could toss but I needed to look through one more time. The new phone list was taped to the pull out drawer so that I could find it easily and so that no one else would be able to walk away with it!

But this approach went beyond the "messy desk syndrome." As I interviewed successful people, I found that many of our so-called bad habits were instead essential to our success. In my case, juggling several projects at once allowed creative insights to leap from one project to another; spending extra minutes talking through a problem with a team member might make me a few minutes late for a meeting, but it helped to restore a relationship between two key people on my staff. Daydreaming in the middle of a meeting or a project seemed to rest my mind so that a great idea could be born, and going off on mind tangents, though it confused some people, seemed to be part of the way my mind wove together a creative new pattern of opportunities. But in all of these examples, I would have gotten bad marks in effective time management because I didn't follow the rules.

I became convinced that somewhere down the line people had created a bunch of great time principles that worked for the factories and industries of the nineteenth century, but that needed revising for the creative worker of the 1990s.

In Part One of this book, my partner Duane Trammell and I will be asking you to rethink your own perception of time. We'll show you how our understanding of time has evolved, and how we have discounted impor-tant ways of viewing time that fly in the face of clockbound efficiency.

In Part Two, we'll help you to assess your personal time manage-ment style and will give you ways to make time management work for you. We will also explore a neglected key to good time management that is usually not seen as a vital enhancer of productivity and quality—*play*.

Finally, in Part Three, you will learn how to add more quality time into every aspect of your life by changing how you think about time. And you don't have to be limited to only twenty-four hours a day. We'll show you some amazing ways to slow down, get curious, regroup, and learn new skills. As a result, you will be able to accomplish much more while improving the balance in your life. This book will help you focus on and improve your "top line"—the quality and joy in your life—as you improve the bottom line and become more productive.

Ann McGee-Cooper

A Note About Gender

We strongly believe in diversity and want to help eliminate the institutional "-isms" such as racism, sexism, and ethnocentrism that are rooted so deeply in the structure and fabric of society. Such biased viewpoints consciously or unconsciously exclude people who are different. Written material commands a power of its own; for that reason, in writing our book, we worked closely with our editor to examine gender references.

It was easy to make third-person-singular text references gender-inclusive. But when it came to direct quotations of famous people from the past, we encountered a problem. Conventional writing rules tell us not to tamper with direct quotations, so we were left with two choices: to use the quotes as they were (which often excluded any mention of women) or to use only quotes that were recently written or nonspecific as to gender. If we used the historical quotes as they were, we would be participating in sending the subtle message that women are less important than their male counterparts. If we only quoted people from the present who were diversity-conscious, we would miss out on some good wisdom from the past.

We didn't like either alternative, so we created a third one. Even though we have quoted people who lived and wrote in a time when "men" was used to refer to both men and women, we have taken the liberty of broadening these references as a reminder that each of us matters. To keep the integrity of the original words of the speaker, we have put in brackets any words we have added.

If this jolts the reader or interrupts the flow of the quote, it may serve as a reminder of how long the gifts of women have been ignored.

TIME BANDITS

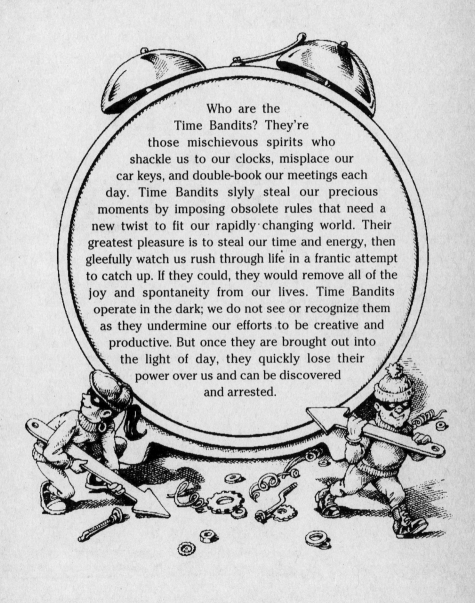

Who are the
Time Bandits? They're
those mischievous spirits who
shackle us to our clocks, misplace our
car keys, and double-book our meetings each
day. Time Bandits slyly steal our precious
moments by imposing obsolete rules that need a
new twist to fit our rapidly·changing world. Their
greatest pleasure is to steal our time and energy, then
gleefully watch us rush through life in a frantic attempt
to catch up. If they could, they would remove all of the
joy and spontaneity from our lives. Time Bandits
operate in the dark; we do not see or recognize them
as they undermine our efforts to be creative and
productive. But once they are brought out into
the light of day, they quickly lose their
power over us and can be discovered
and arrested.

PART
One

HOW CLOCKS BECAME KING

Traditional time management was created to make factories more efficient. Creative thinking was seen not only as unimportant, but also as counterproductive. It would slow down the assembly-line output if workers stopped to ask questions, make suggestions, or simply vary their routine. Thus, workers' efficiency was evaluated on the basis of their conformity.

Factory efficiency introduced the importance of clock time. Since everyone had to be in place for the assembly line to begin, workers wore watches, punched a time clock, and learned to think in terms of units of time—seconds, minutes, hours, days, weeks, vacations, holidays, sick time, and so on. Monochronic time was born. The clock was the single measure of how time was "kept."

The goals of today's business are not only efficiency and productivity, but quality, flexibility, market differentiation, and innovation. These goals require thinking that is not timebound—they happen when they happen, not according to the hands on the clock. They are polychronic in nature, with many complex factors affecting the way time is used. As robotics and high-speed computers master the "efficiency" part of business, people's minds and creative ideas are becoming the appreciating asset of the 1990s. Yet we are still ascribing the same value to monochronic time skills instead of valuing people who are skilled at polychronic time management.

Creative thinkers are divergers by nature. In order to get the best of their innovative thinking ability, we must allow and encourage them to use time differently to generate and nurture the breakthrough ideas. This will require a reengineering of time management with a newly understood appreciation of some lost time skills.

breaking FREE OF THE Assembly-Line MENTALITY

1

❝I must govern the clock, not be governed by it.**❞**

—Golda Meir

❝[A] mind stretched to a new idea never goes back to its original dimensions.**❞**

—Oliver Wendell Holmes, Jr.

❝Technology [is] the knack of so arranging the world that we don't have to experience it.**❞**

—Max Frisch, *Homo Faber*

e take our current sense of time for granted, assuming that we think of time as people have always thought of it. But in fact the Industrial Revolution also brought with it a revolution in the way people in the West think of and respond to time. The growth of factories meant that people needed to be in place at a particular time ready to join together in a single opera-tion. Before this, people who worked together coordinated themselves in different ways. Much earlier, people sang as they rhythmically pulled on the oars of large sailing vessels. Or they may have swung a scythe to a harvesting song to make the work go easier. Sometimes field-workers sang together as they walked out to the fields or home to the hearth. Adding song, which often expressed deep feelings to the rhythms of monotonous labor, was a natural way to create balance.

FACTORY WHISTLES AND POCKET WATCHES

With the Industrial Revolution, we not only decided that everyone must be in place to begin work at the same time, but that to be efficient, work must be done without distractions. If your job was to put identical widgets into identical holes hundreds of times each day, you did it to the clang of machinery. Such routine bores, hypnotizes, then ultimately atrophies the brain. When this kind of work became widespread, people accepted routine jobs as a necessary evil—as they accepted the importance of learning to be prompt.

Pocket watches became common. For the first time in history, many people owned and carried watches. As long as the economy was primarily agricultural, people lived in rhythm with the sun's rising and setting, the seasons, their own bodies' signals, and the needs of the environment. With the rise of the factory, they were encouraged to ignore what their own bodies, intuition, and common sense told them. They were given the message, "You can't stop because your back is tired or your brain is bored." For the factory to function efficiently, every worker had to keep pace.

In his book *The Third Wave*, Alvin Toffler writes that public schools, which developed at the same time as the Industrial Revolution, supported this new mentality by rewarding five behaviors essential to good factory workers: be prompt, be mindlessly obedient, don't question authority, learn to tolerate repetition, and don't expect to enjoy your work—work is simply what must be done.

REPLACING HANDWORK WITH MACHINERY

It is interesting to note that before the Industrial Revolution, craftspeople identified with and took pride in their work. Ar-

5

tisans spent hours making their products beautiful and graceful as well as functional. Look at hand-carved furniture, pottery bowls with elegant painted designs, water pitchers hammered from metal into fanciful shapes—all essentially useful and functional objects, but made with love and individuality by people who took satisfaction from their la-

bor. Skills were passed down from generation to generation, with the family's name tied to the quality of the work. Notice the characteristics of holistic thinking and balance that are woven into this way of working.

A craftsperson worked on a particular piece until it was completed to his or her satisfaction. Speed was not nearly as impor-

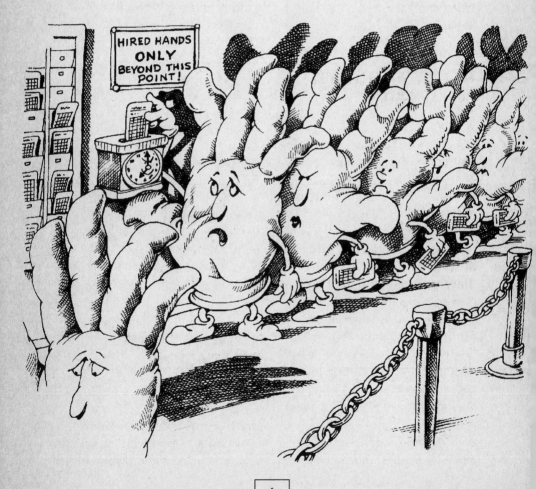

tant as was the experience of holistic excellence. There was no rigid separation between work and play. A barn raising was held when a neighbor needed a new barn, and the community joined in building it. They danced, ate, and celebrated together afterward. Evenings were spent working on crafts combined with music, storytelling, and learning. Square dancing, parlor music, sewing bees, reciting or reading poetry, and other ways of learning and expanding the imagination were seen as fun and were the norm in many cultures. In fact, to be considered cultured, a person was expected to have at least one way of entertaining others—whether by music, storytelling, games, or other skills. Everyone was expected to develop these social graces, and most did.

BREAKING THE WORLD INTO PIECES

Today, in our assembly-line mentality, we have broken the world into either-or boxes. We have become consumers and audiences who expect to be entertained by others. Most of us have lost our capacity to entertain ourselves, not to mention the ability to entertain others. We expect someone else to provide us with a job, forgetting that not so very long ago, many people were their own employers, whose main job was providing for themselves and their families. Almost everyone began work early in life, sharing the satisfaction of contributing to the family and the community and of learning the craft or trade that had been passed down in the family.

I realize that I am generalizing and idealizing a bit about the past, but I encourage you to look for patterns. The patterns that are relevant to our new perspective of time are those that relate to *synchronized time*. Synchronized time encourages us to think that in order to be successful, we need to be prompt, coordinated with the work time of others, and polarized in our thinking. Devotion to synchronized time makes us think in terms of right and wrong, good and bad—and to believe that there is only one right way to do things.

With Frederick Winslow Taylor, the father of time-and-motion studies, came a new belief in one right way to do each task. Workers were called "hired hands" and were valued for their unquestioning obedience. They were taught not to think for themselves, but to "just do as you are told!"

7

Organizations were based on a hierarchy consisting of those who think and those who blindly obey. A good employee was loyal, punctual, and consistent. To question authority or the established standard routine was seen as disruptive behavior or labeled as troublemaking. Simplistic values were quoted: There's one right answer to each question. A person is either good or bad. Being good means conforming to standards.

Standardization became the new ideal. If a person did not fit the standard, he or she was not acceptable. To be different from the standard was rejected on the assembly line. Very soon, to be different from society's standards, whether in IQ, dress, or behavior, would label a person a "reject."

Even as we were learning to make four billion chairs exactly the same by using factories, machines, and assembly lines, it became prestigious to own hand-carved chairs, carefully crafted by people who in all likelihood marched to their own drummer, worked in rhythm with their own bodies, and provided their own quality assurance. Think of the paradox that began to develop. Learning to think and live in paradox is part of the benefit to be gained from the collection of insights in this book. We don't have to decide between the benefits of a monochronic, synchronized world and those of a polychronic, holistic world. By carefully choosing and balancing options, we can enjoy the benefits of both ways of being.

> 66
>
> *Ordinary people think merely how they will spend their time; [a person] of intellect tries to use it.*
>
> —Arthur Schopenhauer
> *Aphorisms on the Wisdom of Life*
>
> 99

IS THERE VALUE IN NOT BEING ON SCHEDULE?

In the past three hundred years, we have gone from a world made up of unique cultures that responded to their own situations, needs, and instincts to a world that places a high value on

8

conformity, consistency, and a mechanized way of doing things. This change has had a heavy influence on our perception of and response to time.

I am not saying that synchronization, punctuality, and consistency are bad or less valuable than earlier ways. I am suggesting that by focusing single-mindedly on these new industrial values, we lost sight of the value of our earlier processes. It was then that we began to become "half-brained," less complete than we have the potential of being. We squelched the uniqueness of the individual in favor of the speed needed for mass production and conformity. And we began to use people as if they were machines, turning off their brains in the process, teaching them *not* to search for better ways, and expecting them to work fifteen-hour shifts until they dropped.

In a more enlightened approach to time management, we are inviting you to discover some new values. Granted, there are times when punctuality, obedience, and repetition are important, but they may not help you meet your goals in today's world. Sacrilegious as it may sound, there are situations in which "wasting time" on a new idea, questioning a policy or procedure (although it may slow down the bureaucratic assembly line), going backward to learn from what went wrong, or stopping to have fun and renew yourself when the pressure is greatest are the most important skills.

But becoming comfortable with this way of thinking requires suspending synchronicity (clock time) for a while and learning how to flow with intuitive time based on your own personal internal clock. It sounds easy, but you'll learn in the next chapter that society sends us a different message.

There are times when punctuality, obedience, and repetition are important, but they may not help you meet your goals in today's world.

9

AN *Epidemic* OF HURRY SICKNESS

66 Just as Pavlov's dogs learned to salivate inappropriately, we have learned to hurry inappropriately. Our sense of urgency is set off not by a real need to act quickly, but through learned cues. Our 'bells' have become the watch, the alarm clock, the morning coffee, and the hundreds of self-inflicted expectations that we build into our daily routine. The subliminal message from the watch and the clock is: time is running out; life is winding down; please hurry. **99**

—Dr. Larry Dossey, *Space, Time & Medicine*

66 My two-year-old son Cole has a working vocabulary of seven words . . . two of them are 'hurry' and 'go.' **99**

—Tracie Reveal, Communications Specialist
Electronic Data Systems

*h*urry sickness

is a term we first learned from the work of Dr. Larry Dossey. In his book, *Space, Time & Medicine,* Dr. Dossey writes, "The perceptions of passing time that we observe from our external clocks cause our *internal* clocks to run faster. . . . [Hurry sickness then is] expressed as heart disease, high blood pressure, or depression of our immune function, leading to an increased susceptibility to infection and cancer."

Hurry sickness is a metaphor for all those illnesses brought on or exacerbated by stress, rush, and constant pressure. Tension headaches, ulcers, and some forms of arthritis can be linked to the flood of adrenaline that results from interpreting life as overlapping crises that demand a heroic response from us without rest or joy. In short, hurry

sickness is habitual, unnecessary, or compulsive rushing that leads to the speeding up of our natural body functions, ultimately damaging our health. We are caught in an epidemic of rushing as an end in itself and, no longer aware of other options, we cannot escape.

So how did it happen that we evolved from memorable childhood moments of lingering, dawdling, and aimlessly daydreaming into an adulthood of rushing from work to home to entertainment events that we often leave early to be first out of the parking lot? As children, we grew up hurrying to keep pace with the longer legs of adults. Once we experienced the shame connected with being slow, none of us wanted to be the last through the door or part of the slow-reading group in school. At the end of recess, we ran to be first in line, and we were praised in gym class for running the fastest. The first student to raise his or her hand got to answer the teacher's question and was recognized as the bright one with a "quick" mind. Slow students were labeled learning-disabled. We picked up dozens of overt and covert messages signaling our society's praise for speed and disdain for anything slower.

As adults, we often sigh with disapproval, tap our feet impa-

What Does Hurry Sickness Look Like in Our Lives?

1 We rush to be first whether we need to or not. As a matter of principle, we press to be first off the airplane even though we know we will just stand and wait with the others once we get to the baggage claim.

2 We press forward, inch by inch, bumper to bumper, in gridlock traffic, incensed if anyone cuts ahead of us even though our lives won't be changed by the five minutes we may "save," once we reach our destination.

3 We finish each other's sentences and rush ahead of the story to guess the ending, never really hearing the message because we are already elsewhere.

4 We skip breakfast or lunch to "save time" or eat on the go.

5 We drum our fingers impatiently or glance frequently at our watch to signal our displeasure at having to wait.

6 We use a new tape recorder that speeds voices up twice as fast so we can listen to tapes in half the time.

7 Our children are scheduled as heavily as we are, every moment of the day and weekend, with soccer practice, after-school clubs, or computer camps.

8 Suddenly, twenty years have rushed through our lives almost unnoticed as we look back at our grown children and wonder where the time went.

tiently, or shake our heads with frustration at those who move with anything less than speed and focus. We have learned to eat on the run; read, shave, and talk on the phone while driving; talk faster; and sleep less. Reading was once a pastime we savored, as we lost ourselves in a consuming novel, biography, or anthology of poetry; now, speed reading, the faster the better, is seen as a more coveted skill.

Our forms of entertainment have gone from slow to fast. Instant replays keep audiences entertained between football plays. And if politicians can't explain their platform for reforming a nation in fifteen seconds or less, we lose interest, switch channels, and go on to something else. Accustomed to "factoids," single-sentence bits of trivia, and short-burst commercials, we find anything longer than a half-hour sitcom beyond our tolerance as we rush both to keep up and to increase the pace any way we can.

Business has picked up on our addiction to speed, discovering that a marketing edge awaits those who can provide products and services faster with greater convenience. In the corporate world, the phrase "chasing business" signals the spreading epidemic infecting our thinking, as we rush in all directions at once, as fast as we can, to "get ahead of the competition." Hurry sickness may be inevitable in an economy where "the early bird gets the worm." My editor made me aware that the speed with which publishers need to respond to book proposals has increased exponentially. She said:

"The decision to take a couple of days to circulate and discuss a proposal can lead to losing it. Someone else can make a preemptive bid before you can reach a group decision. Agents now take pleasure in telling editors, 'Oh, you're the third *to call.'"*

The fax machine has increased our ability to send and receive messages from weeks or days to seconds. Prescription eyeglasses that used to require a two-week wait are now yours in less than an hour. Would you believe that there is even a drive-through funeral parlor where you can view the dead and pay your last respects without turning off the motor or "taking the time" to get out of your car?

While technology and speed help us in most situations and generally make life more convenient, we have begun to apply the "faster is better" operating rule to every aspect of our lives, including areas where it isn't helpful for us to hurry.

HURRY SICKNESS SPREADS TO JAPAN

A new legal issue is moving to the front of Japan's national concerns. Widows are bringing lawsuits against their husbands' employers for *karoshi,* a term meaning death from overwork. According to an article by Gayle Hanson in *Insight on the News,* "After forty years of corporate calisthenics, during which Japan pumped its way to the top of the international money markets, the nation has stopped at the water cooler to ask itself, 'Are we having fun yet?'"

Japanese corporate culture typically has included intense loyalties and very long hours.

Employees typically haven't taken paid holidays and vacations even when they are entitled to them. But now the Japanese are beginning to wonder whether the price of long hours with no time off is worth it.

According to Atsuki Onaga, a staff member at the government-funded Leisure Research and Development Center, "'We knew that the most pressing need for the future was to teach the Japanese how important leisure is. . . . What people need are meaningful and healthy activities in their lives.'" In 1987, following a proposal from the Center, the government officially shortened the work week from forty-eight to forty hours. However, changing the culture is quite another matter.

"DOING" VERSUS "BEING"

Dr. Meyer Friedman and Dr. Ray H. Rosenman write in their book, *Type A Behavior and Your Heart*, "Type A persons have hurry sickness. Their lives are oriented around goals, deadlines, and objectives, which they seem to react to in a driven fashion." I often recognize these symptoms in my own behavior.

One Sunday evening recently, my husband, Larry, and I took a long walk. I confessed to feeling depressed and as I searched behind my heaviness, I felt I had wasted a precious weekend. "I have nothing to show for my time," I heard myself say. True, I had taken long walks, enjoyed several naps, made love, and watched the sun rise and set. But I hadn't painted, read, gardened, or "accomplished" anything. Larry was puzzled, then amused. "Ann," he said, "that's what 'being' time is all about. You drive yourself so hard that when you stop doing and balance by simply being, you start feeling guilty." Suddenly, it hit me. I am so addicted to goals and accomplishments that I felt empty, wasteful, and as if I was being cheated when there was no visible or specific outcome.

In this experience, I learned the value of recruiting a learning partner to support me through my transition to valuing "being" time. I might never have recognized the flaw in my response without another person mirroring it back to me. I had gotten so good at doing, accomplishing, and setting and reaching goals that I not only forgot how to enjoy just being, I also lost my identity to this compulsive master. Now I had an opportunity to balance my dedication to doing with an equal commitment to being— learning to let go, relax, coast, live in the moment, and simply breathe deeply and be fully alive.

As Dr. Larry Dossey wrote in a recent letter to me, "There are many kinds of healing events which come about not by *doing* but by *being*. Adopting a psychological state of cooperation with what is—acceptance, alignment, attunement—sometimes precedes radical, sudden cures. In healing, we are obsessed with doing, not being. Even new agers are hooked on an incessant variety of activities, although they're different from those used by traditionalists. Few people allow themselves to simply *be*. For us, simply 'being' suggests passivity, which we abhor. And 'emptiness' suggests the void—which for us in the West is akin to being swallowed, or actually dying."

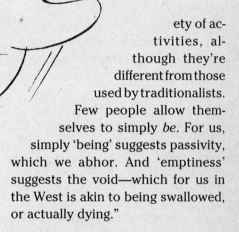

LEARNING TO SLOW DOWN

One of the ways I'm learning to alter my sense of time is by taking off my watch and becoming so engrossed in something I enjoy that I literally lose track of time. This childlike state totally renews me and often brings me back to my senses. The phenomenon is explained best in

Mihaly Csikszentmihalyi's book, *Flow: The Psychology of Optimal Experience.* He describes the state we achieve in work or play or contemplation in which we lose track of time and seem to merge with what we are doing. This heals the split between certain kinds of work and absorbing play and explains why work that holds our attention and allows us to use our creativity may actually make us feel energized and exhilarated by the flow of our own intuitive resources. It also explains why "leisure" activities in which we are bored and uninvolved, such as channel-surfing on TV, can be very depleting.

Meditation, biofeedback, creative visualization, and progressive relaxation are all methods used to effectively alter our sense of losing the battle against fleeting time. In one study by M. Cooper and M. Aygen, subjects taught to meditate were able to lower blood cholesterol levels by an average of 20 percent. Moreover, other aspects of the time syndrome respond: blood pressure, heart and respiratory rate, and the blood levels of insulin, hydrocortisone, adrenaline, and norepinephrine are modified to more desirable levels.

The significance of these observations is inestimable. By "elongating" their time sense, individuals can alter many of the devastating effects of the time syndrome.

In our previous book on increasing personal energy, *You Don't Have to Go Home from Work Exhausted!* we learned the tremendous refreshment that can be enjoyed when we rediscover the way that small children play without the pressure of following rules, fulfilling expectations, keeping score, or judging their performance. This same strategy relieves hurry sickness and offers a renewing balance. For at least this brief time, all urgency and responsibilities vanish as life becomes a collection of magic moments.

William Atkinson, a freelance writer and friend of ours from Murphysboro, Illinois, captures the magic of kid spirit in his personal story:

"After a hard day of 'brain-grinding' writing, the last thing I think I want to do is get physical with my kids—finding more energy to play their games with them.

"However, I have learned—quite accidentally, as a matter of fact—that this can be energy-producing. The accident happened two years ago, when my daughter was seven and my son three. We were getting ready to play a game

> **"**
>
> *Technology is increasing the heartbeat. We are inundated with information. The mind can't handle it all. The pace is so fast now, I sometimes feel like a gunfighter dodging bullets.*
>
> —James Trunzo, Manhattan architect
>
> **"**

of indoor basketball, using various items from around the house.

"As usual, I was ready to delineate the rules and explain them in detail to the kids. However, I was particularly tired that evening, so I ignored the formalities and let the game begin, without saying a word. Luckily, my kids forgot that rules existed and began playing the game without them. Almost immediately, I was ready to jump in and formalize the game. However, again, I was just too tired to protest. So I let things slide, with the 'rules' being made up as we went. Actually, what evolved was no rules, just spontaneous thought and activity.

"Within five minutes, the three of us were having so much fun that we had to stop the game because we were laughing too hard. I felt an incredible rush of energy I hadn't had in twenty years. We finally were able to continue the game— laughing all the way for the next forty-five minutes—until we all dropped from exhaustion.

"Now, I have a new 'rule' when I play with my kids. That rule is to have no rules! Now, when my kids want me to play, I joyously participate, no matter how tired I might be, because I know the free-for-all experience will actually rekindle my energy for the rest of the evening!"

It's possible to get so good at setting and achieving goals that you "accomplish" without ever having lived. Stepping back frequently to reflect on deep values, retreating to nature and becoming absorbed in its tranquil beauty, we realize that time *is* relative, that we can go forward and back, using time to give us new tools and a new perspective.

The solution must honor the paradox, rather than simplistically swinging in only one direction. Technology and competition will continue to push us toward reactive behaviors and attitudes. It is easy to become addicted to the flood of adrenaline stimulated by a constantly rushing, fire-fighting environment. And, symptomatic of an addict, we may feel anxious and under-stimulated without constant crises to challenge us.

To keep our healthy creativity alive and to keep our teams performing at their best, we must intuitively balance quick

Tips to Get Out of Hurry Sickness

pid·dle\ píd-əl \ vi 1: dawdle

put·ter\ pát-ər\ vi 1: to move or act aimlessly or idly

LEARN TO PIDDLE AND PUTTER

1 Find a time over the weekend to take off your watch. Eat, rest, play, and work in response to your body instead of the clock.

2 When possible, choose a weekend morning to sleep late, linger in bed, and read an absorbing novel or enjoy an old movie on television.

3 Go for a drive outside the city on an uncrowded back road. Enjoy the landscape. Purposely go without a destination in mind.

4 Have a picnic at a secluded spot. Take a blanket and some pillows. Lay back, look at the clouds, enjoy unrushed conversation, or take a nap.

5 Take a "stroll" one evening instead of a "power walk."

6 Take a few minutes each day to daydream or fantasize.

7 Linger at the supper table with family and friends, and enjoy the conversation.

8 Limit caffeine—it speeds up your nervous system.

9 Putter in a favorite place—your garage, the kitchen, a hardware store, a garden.

10 Make time for spiritual renewal, solitude, and nature.

response with strategies to help us step back, relax, laugh, let go, enjoy three deep breaths, renew ourselves, and reframe the demands placed on us. There is no magic formula for doing this, but people who respect the value of a holistic approach take quantum leaps beyond those who have become trapped in a hurry-go-round.

Albert Einstein and Thomas Edison, who played often and in childlike ways, model the amazing benefits of balance, as does Southwest Airlines, the only airline that has been in the black for each of the past seven years. Its corporate culture is based on the notion that "people rarely succeed at anything unless they have fun doing it." Its M.B.F.A. approach (Management By Fooling Around) demonstrates the way love and laughter form the foundation of the company's human and financial success.

We each hold the keys to our own prison, while we long to be free. This book will provide you with many fresh insights into why and how you perceive time as you do. Far more important, you will become acutely aware of the hurry sickness rampant in our culture and begin to be part of a healthy alternative.

The next chapter will double your opportunities to experience time more resourcefully. In it, you will discover two opposite and contrasting experiences of time. Monochronic time is measured by clocks and is linear, sequential, and predictable, while polychronic time is complex, relative, and measured more by instinct and intangibles. About half the population think and respond to polychronic time and are therefore seen as poor time managers.

Later chapters will focus on scheduling your time and on the importance of play. Learning the value of balancing work with renewing play, creating more holistic and flexible ways of scheduling your time, and getting as good at your play as you are now at your work are three concepts that will give you some options to cure your hurry sickness.

The last section of the book is designed to show you new ways to open up time in your life. Then it's your challenge to enjoy this newfound time instead of rushing to fill the void with more of the all-too-familiar symptoms of hurry sickness. From learning the fine art of executive neglect to polishing your ability to celebrate anything, anytime, you have great opportunities ahead.

monochronic AND POLYCHRONIC TIME: WOULD SOCRATES OR LINCOLN HAVE SURVIVED IN YOUR COMPANY?

3

> 66 Although monochronic time (M-time) is imposed, learned, and arbitrary, we tend to treat it as if it were built into the universe. The transformative process makes us more sensitive to the rhythms and creative drives of nature and to the oscillations of our own nervous systems. 99
>
> —Marilyn Ferguson, *The Aquarian Conspiracy*

> 66 In monochronic cultures, time is experienced and used in a linear way—comparable to a road extending from the past into the future. ... [Monochronic time] is experienced as being almost tangible: People talk about it as though it were money, as something that can be 'spent,' 'saved,' 'wasted,' and 'lost.' 99
>
> —Edward T. Hall and Mildred Reed Hall
> *Hidden Differences: Doing Business with the Japanese*

23

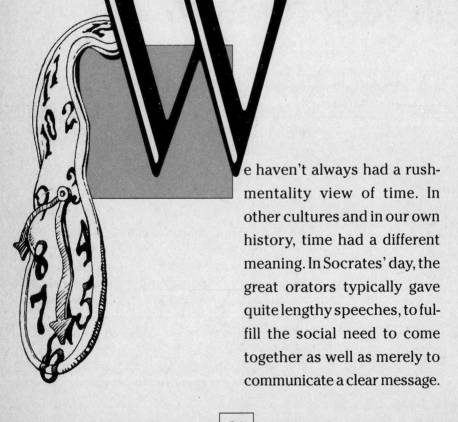

We haven't always had a rush-mentality view of time. In other cultures and in our own history, time had a different meaning. In Socrates' day, the great orators typically gave quite lengthy speeches, to fulfill the social need to come together as well as merely to communicate a clear message.

In ancient Greek culture, people who were invited to spend an evening with friends arrived at whatever time their journey allowed and left when the visit seemed complete.

When Abraham Lincoln delivered his now-famous Gettysburg Address, most of his listeners assumed that he had disgraced himself. Long speeches were the norm at this time. The Gettysburg Address took only a few minutes to deliver, and its brevity was an affront to those present. Lincoln was not concerned. He said what he had to say and sat down.

Winston Churchill used this same strategy of surprise to capture the attention of his audience in a commencement address at Harrow School in 1941. He is said to have stepped up to the podium, put his cane aside, looked deeply into the eyes of his audience, and declared, "Never give in, never give in, never, never, never, never—in nothing, great or small, large or petty—never give in except to convictions of honor and good sense." And with that, he left the podium. His break with tradition only served to emphasize his message; it captured the imagination of everyone who was present and the generations to come who would hear this story.

There are many different ways to perceive and evaluate time. In our culture, we are locked into a very narrow view of effective time management. We think that compressing the largest number of things into the smallest number of minutes is the most efficient way, but in fact we may be lessening the quality of our work, narrowing our span of vision, increasing our tension and worry, and cutting off the possibility of creativity and satisfaction in work by this narrow view. We can significantly increase our effectiveness if we can broaden our awareness of the different ways of perceiving time.

OUTSIDE CLOCKS VERSUS INSIDE CLOCKS

There are two opposite ways of viewing time: *monochronic* and *polychronic*. Monochronic time refers to linear time—time that is measured by the clock and typically decided in advance. When you function in monochronic time, you reward and appreciate promptness, speed, brevity, and punctuality. *Shorter* and *faster* mean *better*. On the other hand, in the polychronic approach, time is related to many complex factors; decisions are typically made intuitively, in the moment, as events play out. This is a more complex system in that time is not considered to be absolute, but relative. When you function in polychronic time, you reward and appreciate flexibility, intuition, dedication, inspiration, imagination, and many other factors. Trust, bonding, pleasure, and quality of life influence your decisions.

You can apply monochronic skills and thinking to most predictable tasks. For example, you probably can predict fairly accurately how long it takes you to dress for work, or boil an egg, or type six pages. In contrast, ask yourself how long it takes to fall in love, gain a new client's trust, solve a computer problem, create a new product or service, resolve a bitter argument to the satisfaction of both parties, or gain the total support of your team. These are far more complex polychronic issues, which typically are not predictable in advance. Note that most of them deal with people, feelings, and intangibles. In fact, if you stay too focused on the clock, you can actually slow down or sabotage your goal. The implied message— "Time and speed are more important than people, trust, consensus, and a win-win agreement"—can heavily or permanently discount both your motives and the relationship.

This issue has become a major barrier in American–Pacific Rim business relationships. We Westerners honor others by acting quickly, getting to the point, and pushing for quick closure. In Asian cultures, honor is shown by developing long-term relationships, listening, and keeping the dialogue open. This is a classic mismatch of monochronic versus polychronic processing.

Some professions require their employees to work primarily in monochronic time. Airline

> ## 66
> *Life forms illogical patterns. It is haphazard and full of beauties which I try to catch as they fly by, for who knows whether any of them will ever return?*
>
> —Margot Fonteyn
>
> ## 99

gate agents, assembly-line workers, cab and bus drivers, and cashiers all are governed by the clock. Watching the clock and staying punctual are essential in these fields, where faster *is* better. Other professions are not as closely bound to monochronic time and require instead a sensitivity to polychronic time. Although they involve time requirements, schedules, appointments, and deadlines, careers in teaching, counseling, sales, and the arts require you to schedule the task to fit the time.

The more you deal directly with people, the more polychronic you must become. Many managers make the mistake of refusing to shift their time perception. They continue to push for speed alone and consequently lose the trust and support of their team. Slowing down and listening to other people's ideas, problems, proposed solutions, and concerns might give them a greater advantage in the long term.

For example, while you will typically schedule a certain amount of time for a business meeting, sometimes an important topic takes longer than planned. Rather than cutting the meeting off promptly at 3:00 P.M. to stay on schedule, it may be to your advantage to deal with what is currently on the table and let other things slide for the moment. You probably are familiar with unplanned but important interruptions in your schedules. You plan to leave the office at 9:00 A.M. for a site visit, but at 8:55 A.M., an important client calls and wants to share an extended conversation. If you take the call, your departure will be delayed. If you don't take the call, your client will be upset. By asking your secretary to call the site and let the people waiting know you will be delayed, you allow them to shift their plans. Or you might ask your client to let you return the call from your car phone within five minutes as you drive to the site. The switch to polychronic time (a time resolution that is natural) allows you to flex your schedule as the need arises.

OTHER CULTURES, OTHER TIMES

Edward T. Hall, renowned anthropologist, lecturer, and consultant on international business, and his partner, researcher Mildred Reed Hall, help us to realize that there are many kinds of time systems in the world. In their book, *Understanding Cultural Differences,* they offer a chart of the classic differences between monochronic and poly-chronic time systems, shown below. As you review this chart, think about how you prefer to work and live. Though they have related these classic differences to cultures as a whole, we have found that the same patterns seem to apply to individuals.

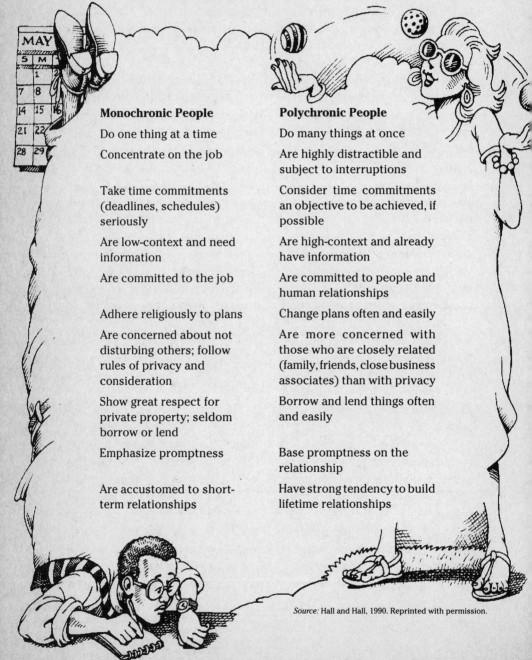

Monochronic People	Polychronic People
Do one thing at a time	Do many things at once
Concentrate on the job	Are highly distractible and subject to interruptions
Take time commitments (deadlines, schedules) seriously	Consider time commitments an objective to be achieved, if possible
Are low-context and need information	Are high-context and already have information
Are committed to the job	Are committed to people and human relationships
Adhere religiously to plans	Change plans often and easily
Are concerned about not disturbing others; follow rules of privacy and consideration	Are more concerned with those who are closely related (family, friends, close business associates) than with privacy
Show great respect for private property; seldom borrow or lend	Borrow and lend things often and easily
Emphasize promptness	Base promptness on the relationship
Are accustomed to short-term relationships	Have strong tendency to build lifetime relationships

Source: Hall and Hall, 1990. Reprinted with permission.

Those of us who are divergent and flexible in our approach to life and problem solving are more likely to naturally process in polychronic ways, and those of us who are more convergent and structured in our thinking styles are more apt to process monochronically.

In *Hidden Differences—Doing Business with the Japanese,* Hall and Hall give the following definitions of monochronic and polychronic time: "Monochronic time (M-time) means *paying attention to and doing only one thing at a time.* Polychronic time (P-time) means *being involved with many things at once*" (italics added). Understanding both the monochronic and polychronic systems of time is helpful in dealing with cultures and individuals who process time differently from ourselves.

The American culture functions as though its monochronic time system were universal, but such is not the case. Western cultures such as the United States, Switzerland, Germany, and Scandinavia are dominated by monochronic time while the French, Latin Americans, and Arabs, for instance, use polychronic time. Hall and Hall maintain that the Japanese combine both systems: "In their dealings with foreigners and their use of technology, they are quite monochronic; in every other way, especially in interpersonal relations, they are polychronic."

HIGH-CONTEXT AND LOW-CONTEXT CULTURES

The Halls describe two contrasting cultural patterns that they term *high-context* and *low-context.* In a high-context culture, people stay in close touch constantly, so most of the background information about others is already known. Few details are needed for any one communication because they have already been shared. Japanese, Arab, French, and Latin American cultures are high-context.

In *Understanding Cultural Differences,* Hall and Hall state: "Low-context people include Americans, Germans, Swiss, Scandinavians, and other northern Europeans; they compartmentalize their personal relationships, their work, and many aspects of day-to-day life. Consequently, each time they interact with others they need detailed background information. . . . High-context people are apt to become impatient and irritated when low-context people insist on giving them information they don't need. Conversely, low-

context people are at a loss when high-context people do not provide *enough* information."

How does this relate to time management? Have you ever been told to save time by limiting your communication to only one page? This works wonderfully if you are communicating with a high-context person. But it will fail if you are communicating with a low-context person who will only trust your information if you provide supporting data to prove you have done your homework.

We are often told that the secret to good meetings is to have an agenda that is circulated in advance—to fix time allotted to each agenda item, stick to the agenda, and so on. The Halls teach us that for the French, Japanese, or any other high-context people, a tight, fixed agenda can be an encumbrance, even an insult to their intelligence. Most, if not all, of those present have a pretty good idea of what will be discussed beforehand. As they state in *Hidden Differences,* "Adherence to a rigid agenda and the achievement of consensus represent opposite goals and do not mix."

Some Americans are high-context people. They understand the big picture and go to meetings with an open mind, expecting to learn from others. They feel that the purpose of meetings is to allow time for agendas to emerge, be heard, and be resolved, and they believe that these agendas come not from one person but from everyone present. For such people, too much structure blocks the flow of communication and trust; they obtain their best results when they allow an intuitive agenda to emerge naturally, with high trust and openness. They believe in their ability to listen intuitively and achieve consensus by involving each member of the group. They do not measure a good meeting by how quickly it adjourns but rather by how much is shared, resolved, and agreed upon, even though the meeting may have gone well

past the time allotted to it. Can you see how shortsighted we may become if we have only one system for structuring our time? We may please half the population but organize ourselves and our business teams in such a way that we fail miserably when we attempt to deal with other cultures and even with those other valuable people in our own culture and families.

This dichotomy may also spill over into other areas of time management. High-context people devote a lot of time to keeping up with the many extraneous details of other people's lives. They may chat about family, hobbies, and civic groups. This can seem like a waste of time to low-context people, yet it is a way of gathering all sorts of related information that can contribute to more in-depth decision making and problem solving down the road. Our firm's involvement with organizations that do business internationally reinforces what we had previously learned from our work with people who have become more balanced and self-actualized as individuals and as members of teams and families. If we open our ways of working and living and learn to appreciate the value of other approaches that seem counterproductive because they are opposite from ours, we can gain the benefits of both. But if we attempt to pit one against the other to learn which is best, we will miss the benefits of this global and unlimited synergy.

MOTHERS ARE POLYCHRONIC BY NECESSITY

In our society, women who are homemakers and mothers are forced to be polychronic. Just try to get a family of three small children dressed and in the car by a certain time. The baby throws up or wets his diaper just as you are ready to leave. The dog knocks over the goldfish bowl and you frantically rescue fish, ignoring the cut on your finger from the broken glass. Your day is planned, and then the washing machine overflows on the new carpet. This kind of life-style encourages polychronic thinking. You must maintain very flexible time expectations just to keep your sanity. Keeping strictly to a preplanned clock schedule is simply impossible.

Business, on the other hand, has traditionally forced both women and men into monochronic time. Being punctual is a top priority. If you arrive late to a sales call or client meeting, you might as well forget it. Meeting appointments and deadlines is an essential quality to earning respect and credibility among your peers.

When you think about it, much of the business world runs on a monochronic schedule. The train runs every seven minutes; the stock exchange opens and closes at a certain time; the office is closed for lunch from noon to 1:00 P.M. Of course, many factors aren't this reliable, but the outside structure gives the illusion of predictability, and that illusion slips into our assumptions about life in general. We act as if we believe that all of life can be predicted in advance and kept on a schedule. Sometimes we even try to take our monochronic focus home. The response to this can best be understood by the reply of a fourteen-year-old to his executive parent: "I'm not just another agenda item for you to check off on your list of to-do's."

The more you work with and are responsible for small children and people in general, the less monochronic thinking will work for you. The more you work with *things,* which can be controlled and predicted, the more successfully you can use monochronic time. This may blind you to the need to expand your thinking about time.

SHOULD WE THROW AWAY OUR CLOCKS?

Why does all of this matter? If you judge and evaluate yourself only in terms of monochronic time, although your responsibilities require polychronic skills, you will be forever frustrated unless you learn the fine art of blending both approaches into a far more successful whole. If you judge yourself and others simply on the basis of whether a specific schedule was kept, you may be overlooking essential elements in the process.

In many cases, people who take longer on the phone, in meetings, and in person are high-context people who may be sensing intuitively that some unspoken issues still need airing. People who concentrate only on rushing to closure are more inclined to miss opportunities to resolve problems, and they may be sending a subconscious signal that time is more important than people or relationships. This can be an expensive and unnecessary mistake. Larry Hart, CEO of International Technology Corporation, Torrance, California, says:

"I have found the following approach helpful when dealing with monochronic and polychronic tasks. On the evening before, I identify the four or five tasks that must be done for sure. If they require input or participation from others, I schedule appointments in advance. It's dangerous to rely on 'just dropping in' to their office or 'just calling them.' If they are unavailable, I can't get the tasks done and I miss the deadline. That's the monochronic side of planning.

"But there are other kinds of tasks that I also work on in the course of the day. These are tasks that I need to think about and incubate. I write them down, too, but I don't schedule specific time for them. The best metaphor I can think of to explain this polychronic form of time is a computer's multitask processing. I can open up three or four applications on top of one another. Granted, I can only work on the one on top, but I can switch back and forth more easily if they are already up and running. The to-do tasks are like that, too. They are in the background of my mind, ready to pull up for processing when I want to work on them."

Let me share a few other interesting examples of how some of our clients and friends have blended the best of both time approaches to deal with polychronic issues in a monochronic world.

Professionals Share Their Insights

- *Doris Denny, secretary to Tom Blakey, then vice president of Texas Power & Light,* opened time for me when none was available on Tom's heavily monochronic schedule. She struck up a bargain with me: "I'll get you in to see him for ten minutes if you promise to get him out the door at noon for his board meeting."

- *The chairman of a large corporation* had many important, unexpected polychronic situations to resolve; they usually came in the form of urgent phone calls from city officials just as he was leaving for other important meetings. He coached his secretary to step over to the meeting and encourage the participants to begin without him until he could get free.

Tips for Polychronic Situations with Monochronic Expectations

☞ **I**f an appointment is running over and someone is waiting, politely interrupt and let the other person know that you would like to continue the discussion but have another appointment. Ask if it would be possible to resume the discussion at a meeting in the future.

☞ **C**ommunicate at the start of a meeting the amount of time you have set aside. Say, "I have ten minutes before I must leave for the airport. Can I answer your question in that amount of time, or would it be better to call you once I'm in the air?" or "We have one hour for this staff meeting, and we must have a decision at the end of our time together. Let's collect an agenda of our concerns about the product and set some approximate time allotments to help move us through so that we don't take up all of our time on just one issue."

☞ **A**djust the percentage of perfection required on the task. If an unchangeable monochronic deadline is approaching fast, work with your polychronic partners to redefine how "polished" a new idea must be to present it to the group.

☞ **S**huffle the deck if you need more time to complete a project. Quickly assess other items on your list that might be dropped, delegated, delayed, or done with less polish to allow the extra time you need.

- *A dentist* schedules "open time" throughout the day to take care of emergencies. He is set up to do his own lab work, so if there are no emergencies, he just gets that much ahead.

- Mary Ann Mayshaw, secretary to Dennis Bernhart, vice president of Hydrocarbon, Fluor Daniel, developed a system to assess which appointments were likely to be poly-

chronic and made sure not to schedule polychronic appointments back-to-back without a cushion of time in case they ran over.

- *A manager at a construction site* has a team of highly creative engineers who enjoy talking for long periods of time about their ideas. He purposely schedules meetings around 4:00 P.M., knowing that the engineers are more likely

Tips for Monochronic Situations with Polychronic Needs

Keep an ongoing dialogue with your team about ways you can create flexible time goals. If you need more time in a meeting, check with others to see if it's possible to stay longer by stopping for a break and calling ahead to shift other changeable appointments.

If you find yourself being driven by the clock on a creative task, take a refreshing break or purposely do something else for a while to remove some of the forced time pressure.

Whenever possible, make it a habit to develop an alternative plan. Keep others informed on matters that might affect them or change, so they can help you make new plans instantly as needed.

When scheduling polychronic tasks or events, do so loosely and approximately. Leave open windows of time between events. (We know of an executive with a calendar that is accessible to everyone on computer who blocks out "appointments" with a fictitious person in order to give himself the polychronic windows he needs.)

Step back from the intensity and pressure of your work several times a day. Totally relax and create a joy break, time to have fun and renew for a moment. (A complete description of joy breaks can be found in Chapter Twelve.) In this more holistic state of mind, you often can discover breakthrough insights. Sometimes you must slow down to go faster.

to come to closure because they are ready to go home. If some want to stay and brainstorm, but others are itching to get out the door, he encourages them to feel free to do either. Great ideas are generated without others feeling trapped.

- *A CEO* often asks her team to table a decision and let it rest for a week or so when she feels that closure came too fast and without the necessary consideration of all factors. This gives her time to let her intuition speak to her, and she finds that better solutions emerge.

Tips for Home Life

- *A dentist friend* found that a source of conflict in his marriage was his monochronic desire to arrive at parties or church "on time" while his wife ran five to twenty minutes late. His solution was to discuss his feelings and needs with her. He enjoyed arriving early enough to socialize, while she needed extra time for grooming and didn't enjoy extended socializing. Since they had two cars, they decided to take both cars when-

ever there was more than a five-minute difference in their departure times. This allowed them both to feel that their needs were being met. On one occasion when the drive took over forty-five minutes, she simply brought her extra makeup and stayed in the car to finish her grooming while he went in to begin enjoying the party.

- *Diane Cory, a mother of three young daughters,* found weekday mornings a continuing battle against the clock; she barked orders while the girls dragged their feet. Then she created a refreshing change. Instead of throwing open the bedroom door, turning on the lights, and yelling "Time to get up!" she lifted her daughters onto her lap one at a time. Cuddling each one for a few minutes in a blanket, she welcomed her into the day, speaking quietly of all the pleasant opportunities waiting for her to enjoy. This extra ten to fifteen minutes each morning made a tremendous difference. The girls got along better, moved happily with their own rhythms, and got ready without their previous struggles. Mornings became pleasant, meaningful times to share and enjoy instead of something to be endured and rushed through.

LEARNING WHEN EACH TIME APPROACH IS CALLED FOR

In our busy world, it is impossible to spend open-ended time on every issue that arises. For that reason, it is important that we learn to use both monochronic and polychronic perspectives. Each perspective can be woefully blind to the many advantages of the other. When they are pitted against each other, each falls short of the long-term benefits that are necessary for successful living, teaming, work, and joyful satisfaction. Yet when they are blended together, a remarkable synergy results, which outproduces either style by far. The key is learning when each approach is appropriate.

Obviously, an airline pilot can't mill around interminably with passengers to make sure

everyone is comfortable, at ease, and psychologically prepared for takeoff. Just as obviously, a parent can't set aside a firm twenty minutes to determine why a youngster is suddenly doing poorly in school. At work, you won't tell a dissatisfied customer you have five minutes to hear a complaint, just as you won't devote your entire afternoon to discussing the pros and cons of changing brands of photocopier paper with the sales representative. Becoming aware of the different ways of looking at time and realizing that you have the power to choose is a giant step toward feeling that you are spending your time as you want to rather than being time's slave. The most important thing is to celebrate any gains you make toward balancing monochronic and polychronic time, even before you get perfect.

But developing an appreciation for polychronic time management first requires understanding and appreciating how the divergent mind works. This will be discussed in Chapter Four.

Divergers
AND CONVERGERS:
BY HELICOPTER,
OR ON FOOT?

39

There are at least two ways to approach life, time, and work. One way is the logical, practical, convergent way: define a task and get it done. The other is the innovative, intuitive, divergent way: define a task, then do something else.

This description may make you laugh—or cry—depending on your own traits and the traits of those you love. The differences in these approaches can cause a great deal of frustration and puzzlement until you understand that each way is valid— they just don't work equally well for all people.

In their book, *Thinking Better,* David Lewis and James Greene describe the following situation:

"Two children get lost in a remote part of the country and a search is mounted to find them. Depending on weather conditions and the type of terrain, the authorities could decide to use either or both of two methods. Groups of rescuers may be sent out on foot to cover the area where the youngsters were last seen. They will probe the undergrowth, hunt diligently through the woods, explore mountain tracks and forest trails, go into caves and climb down ravines as they carry out a detailed and methodical search. At the same time that those foot searchers are scouring the countryside, rescue helicopters might be called in to survey wide areas of the terrain from several hundred feet above."

The authors go on to say that both rescue methods have their advantages and limitations. The pathfinders will cover the ground thoroughly and find the children provided they are looking in the right places. However, this is time-consuming and may bring help too late. The helicopter strategy allows a great deal of ground to be covered rapidly, and if the crews are observant, the children may be found within minutes. However, if the children are hidden beneath trees, in a cave, or in a ravine, the air crew could falsely conclude that they have left the area and move on.

This rescue situation represents the different thinking and problem-solving styles of divergers and convergers. Divergent thinkers scan the big picture, look at a situation from varied, new points of view, generate and gather more facts and ideas, and create a bigger and bigger picture. Divergers enlarge their lives and time commitments.

Convergent thinkers operate in reverse. They narrow the picture down to a smaller, more manageable size and perspective, casting out options and purposely selecting just a few. They zero in on key factors and make choices. Convergers focus and compartmentalize their lives and time commitments.

Many of us find ourselves trapped in the body and mind of a divergent person, so we spend

Comparison of
Divergent and Convergent Thinkers

The Divergent Thinker	The Convergent Thinker
Makes many from one	Makes one from many
Expands	Contracts
Scans the big picture	Zeros in
Skips around	Works step-by-step
Branches out	Narrows down
Does it now!	Is patient, plans for later
Is intuitive	Is logical
Likes open space	Likes certainty
Is comfortable with ambiguity, guesswork, and hunches	Prefers "hard" data and facts
Seeks out as many answers as possible	Seeks single correct answer
Is seen as "scatterbrained"	Is seen as "narrow-minded"

most of our lives frustrated and humiliated when we can't seem to get ourselves to do much of anything "right." Society, business, and tradition tend to favor convergent time management practices. Quick decision making, sequential step-by-step approaches, "hard" data and facts, one answer rather than many— all are qualities celebrated by conventional society. Yet most innovative ideas have come from wandering on tangents, having ambiguous priorities, and using intuitive guesswork—all of which make the divergent thinker very comfortable.

In our research we have found some interesting patterns related to time management that may help you to better understand and appreciate the way the divergent mind works.

JUGGLING SEVERAL TASKS AT ONCE

The divergent person usually tackles many jobs at one

time and hops from one to another. If I work in the yard, I may start by weeding and then begin watering. In a minute, I'll decide to transplant some daisies. If the bed is too hard to dig, I go to the compost pile, but instead of returning with a wheelbarrow filled with compost, I trim around the stepping-stones. After six hours, I have worked all over the yard, yet an observer may be hard-pressed to see my progress. If I were linear and convergent, I would finish the weeding before even considering getting out the hose. But instead, I listen to my body and my mind, which tell me that weeding is making my back hurt and is pretty boring, so I should stand up, stretch, and water for a while. While I'm watering, I notice that the daisies are too crowded, so on to them. To me, this is a logical sequence and a satisfying and creative use of my time. A convergent thinker, however, would be driven bonkers by my system.

Once, in a seminar, a woman explained that on Saturdays she cleaned the house. Her method was to clean a bit in the kitchen, carry something to the bedroom, and, while there, make the bed, hang up a few clothes, and then carry underwear to be hand-washed. She moved from job to job until everything was clean.

Her husband was quite critical, and he insisted that the only way to clean was to completely finish in one room before moving on to the next. This was a clear example of how convergent and divergent styles often cause conflict. I suggested that she invite her husband to clean the house in whatever style suited him—or appreciate the results as she cleaned her way (and appreciate the fact that she was doing the cleaning!).

Juggling several tasks at once takes no more time than doing one task before moving to another. In fact, if you are a divergent thinker, it will probably save you time because you don't have to stop to continually nag yourself about finishing the job!

KEEPING THE CREATIVE JUICES FLOWING

If you typically work on six to eight projects at once, chances are that you are intuitively juggling your work to balance your energy and interests. If divergent thinkers become blocked on one project, we may shift to another. Often, when we are working on the second thing, we understand in a flash what we must do to complete or continue the first project. What seems like a disorganized, misdirected waste of time to the linear, convergent person may be a divergent way of keeping the work going while we are waiting for our brain to produce the insights we need.

We have learned that our brains work on current problems twenty-four hours a day. The very first "Eureka!" came as a result of subconscious processing of a problem. Archimedes, the third-century B.C. Greek mathematician, had been puzzling for days over how to determine whether a gold crown was adulterated with silver. All the concentrated thought he could muster had not solved the problem, but one evening as he stepped into a bath and noticed that the water overflowed, he suddenly realized that the principle of displacement could be used to compare the weights of the crowns. He is said to have jumped from the bath and run naked down the street,

shouting "Eureka! Eureka!" (Greek for "I have found it!").

Even as we sleep, our brains are processing ideas, which is why so many creative "Eurekas" may come through dreams. Elias Howe got the breakthrough idea for the sewing machine when a dream inspired his realization that the hole in a needle could be in the bottom instead of the top. Friedrich Kekulé's dream of a serpent swallowing its tail gave him the idea for the structure of the benzene ring, which was the foundation for organic chemistry. These are just a few examples of breakthrough solutions that came after extended subconscious processing. Learning to shift your efforts and your energy back and forth between projects that demand different kinds of energy and effort can be renewing and highly productive. You also save time because as you become bored or weary, you work more slowly and less creatively and efficiently.

I suspect that this process is very individual. It is critically important to listen to your body and your instincts. What works beautifully for one person tires and frustrates someone else. And don't limit yourself to *either* divergent *or* convergent work styles. Drawing from the benefits of both may significantly ener-gize and improve your productivity and satisfaction. You are in the best position to experiment and discover what can be your own most productive, creative, and efficient work style. Just don't tie your hands by insisting that you complete one project before even considering the next. Be open to many options.

TRUSTING INTUITION

Do you ever find yourself reading a magazine back to front, or perhaps reading a short bit in several articles before settling down to enjoy one complete

It is critically important to listen to your body and your instincts. What works beautifully for one person tires and frustrates someone else.

article? You may even do this with books. I suspect that this browsing approach is a way to turn off your logical brain and invite your intuitive brain to take center stage. I find that I often get a feel for which chapters in a book might give me the greatest payoff by browsing, hit or miss, through the pages before starting to read. It is in this process that I decide whether to read front to back, read every word, or only read certain chapters closely. I may spot-read, skimming along in search of the ideas that are relevant to my interests. Or perhaps my skimming tells me that I need to pay close attention and read the book carefully word for word.

Although some linear, convergent readers might discount the back-to-front approach to magazine reading, for divergent readers, it is a way of sampling the articles to see which of them hold our interest enough for a complete reading. Instead of being crazy and random, this approach makes a lot of sense—to some of us.

THE BEST OF BOTH WORLDS

One of the purposes of this book is to encourage divergent thinkers to discover a rich appreciation for a long-over-looked, ridiculed, and discounted set of gifts. A second purpose is to help convergent thinkers recognize the merits inherent in divergent processes. A third is to encourage convergent and divergent thinkers to discover and create space and appreciation for both ways of working and living. The achievement of strength and balance through combining differences in mutually supportive ways is a tremendous reward for those who are open-minded and creative enough to discover it.

Too often we are inclined to be critical of styles that are different from our own. The convergent thinker is apt to think of the divergent style as too fragmented and open-ended. The divergent thinker is apt to think of the convergent style as too narrow, limiting, and lacking in creativity. In fact, however, few of us are purely convergent or purely divergent— and that kind of purity is not our goal. Our goal is to find the appropriate style for each task, to learn from each other, and to benefit mutually from each other's strengths. Recognizing and understanding these different approaches can help us in all our dealings with other people and in a wide variety of situations. If we know when it is important to keep to a schedule and when it is counterproductive, we will save great amounts of time in the long run, and when we become supportive of and apply the best of both divergent and convergent processes, tremendous gains are made. Not only is more accomplished in less time with higher excellence, but tasks are done with more joy, creativity, and satisfaction. The quality and use of time is transformed. Indeed, one plus one can equal seven when both of these time management approaches are combined synergistically.

> **66**
>
> *Pursue 'mindless' interruptions. . . .*
> *Despite advice to focus and ignore*
> *the extraneous, I applaud the idea*
> *and attempt to follow it.*
> *Practical translation: Allow for*
> *(plan for!) unplanned inter-*
> *ruptions. . . . I often find more*
> *useful information about 'life' in*
> *Section D of USA Today than in*
> *The Wall Street Journal. . . . Most*
> *'ahas,' mundane or grand, come*
> *from the juxtaposition of*
> *surprising streams of information.*
>
> —Tom Peters
>
> **99**

PART
Two

CREATING YOUR OWN TIME MANAGEMENT SYSTEM

Traditional time management rules work wonderfully for some people. They help those people get and stay organized, work predictably within their time frames, and finish projects as they are scheduled. The people for whom these traditional approaches are so successful are those who are convergent and structured in their thinking styles. They rely on their analytical, verbal, and linear skills to bring things together in a "timely" manner.

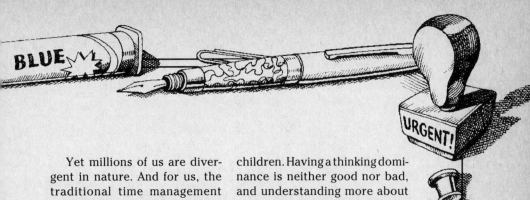

Yet millions of us are divergent in nature. And for us, the traditional time management approach is frustrating, confusing, and counterproductive. The divergent person relies on intuitive knowledge, on spatial and complex relationships, and on creative approaches that can wreak havoc on an orderly, step-by-step plan.

Neither type of thinking is superior to the other. In fact, we all rely on different thinking skills for accomplishing our tasks. However, most of us do have a definite preference, and that preference influences everything we do in life. It influences how we decorate our homes, lead staff meetings, organize our kitchens, plan our vacations, get our work done, and parent our

children. Having a thinking dominance is neither good nor bad, and understanding more about our preferences and differences can help us all relax a little bit.

The key in choosing a time management system lies in learning what kind of thinker you are and choosing a system that works with, rather than against, your personal strengths. The focus of the chapters in this part is on finding ways to use a wider range of thinking skills to their maximum potential. The goal is to become balanced rather than polarized in your thinking. We hope the insights and strategies in these pages will show you how to build your own highly effective, balanced system of time and life management.

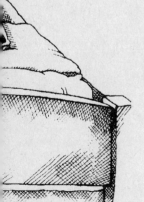

messy DESK OR METICULOUS ORDER: ASSESSING YOUR STYLE

> 66 When you have got a thing where you want it, it is a good thing to leave it where it is. 99
>
> —Sir Winston Churchill

> 66 Creative clutter is better than tidy idleness. 99
>
> —Author unkxnown

> 66 Nobody who can read is ever successful at cleaning out the attic. 99
>
> —Franklin P. Jones

M

uch has been said and written in recent years about the two brain hemispheres. While experts argue about the degree of specialization in the two hemispheres, there is general agreement that they do specialize in different kinds of thinking. In *Left Brain, Right Brain,* Sally Springer and Georg Deutsch write,

"In virtually every approach to the study of hemispheric processes, including approaches using normal individuals, findings support the existence of hemispheric differences."

Several excellent resources on the subject are listed in the Bibliography (see books by Bogen and Gazzaniga, Bogen and Vogel, and Sperry). If you are interested in the neurological and technical aspects of the original research, we suggest that you do a more in-depth study than these pages can allow. For our purposes here, know that we are simplifying and generalizing about some very complex information. If the specifics of the physiology of hemisphericity concern you, simply use the information in this chapter as a metaphor or model for understanding the two opposite ways of processing information.

Over the past thirty years, Roger Sperry, Robert Ornstein, and other scientists have learned a great deal about the specialization of the brain's two frontal hemispheres. In the early 1960s, Roger Sperry began research that confirmed the two hemispheres' separate functions, earning him a Nobel Prize in 1983. In one experiment he studied the brains of epileptic patients whose connection between the left and right hemispheres had been sev-

The secret of geniuses' accomplishments does not lie in what they have, but in how they use their brains.

ered in order to decrease the symptoms of their disease. In this experiment a split-brain patient held a pencil in his right hand but was not allowed to see it. Because the right hand is connected to the left brain hemisphere, the patient could describe the pencil in words. But when he held the same pencil in the opposite hand, which stimulates the right hemisphere, he could not identify it by speech but only by pointing to a picture of it.

Advances in technology now allow us to see inside the brain while we are involved in the thinking process. Powerful new devices peer through the skull and see the brain at work. Included are:

55

- Magnetic resonance imaging, which records detailed images of the brain

- Positron emission tomography, which tracks blood flow (blood flow reflects brain activity)

- The superconducting quantum interference device, which is sensitive to magnetic fields, an indication of brain action

These new devices give us a more detailed and complete picture of the way the two hemispheres function. While earlier studies gave us a beginning understanding of hemispheric specialization on certain tasks, we now know that complex functions like reading, music appreciation, and creative thinking constantly access both hemispheres. The simplified "right-brain" and "left-brain" labels of the seventies and eighties helped us grasp an elementary understanding of the hemispheres, but our current information indicates a much more complex and sophisticated brain system.

Although it is easy to misapply the information on hemisphericity by oversimplifying it, it is significant to know that there are two opposite ways of processing information. By the time

we reach our early twenties, most of us have developed a preferred thinking style. The more we practice our favorite thinking style, the better we get at it and the less likely we are to use opposite thinking abilities. Our perception of time is influenced by our thinking preference; it also controls the way we approach tasks and the stimuli that increase or decrease our productivity.

THE CONNECTION BETWEEN THINKING STYLES AND TIME MANAGEMENT

In order to create a time management system that works for you, you will need to understand what you respond to and what form this response takes. The "Self-Assessment of Thinking Styles and Time Management Skills" on pages 59–64 will help you understand how you process and organize information. It is designed as a teaching tool to raise your self-awareness. *It is not a test.* If you would prefer a more in-depth look, other good instruments are available, such as the Herrmann Brain Dominance Instrument, which is referenced in the Bibliography.

If your score on the self-assessment represents a heavily

SCIENCE
VERSUS
PRACTICALITY

A fascinating debate by academicians and scientists on the one hand, and pragmatists such as educators and business consultants on the other, focuses on the accuracy and integrity of brain- or hemisphere-dominance theories and applications. We all seem to be fascinated to learn more about ourselves, and new labels and explanations for behavioral patterns frequently become fads. When we examine the bias on each side of the argument, we find that each position takes on new meaning; indeed, they may be the two ends of a single paradox instead of two conflicting "truths."

The academic or scientist is trained to look very specifically at a carefully defined area, to control all the variables, and to analyze the hypothesis and make sure it is accurate. The pragmatist is trained to look broadly across many fields of research and to synthesize and test scientific fact by applying it to real situations. The proof of a new "truth" is in the success of its application. This is typically done in very general ways with highly intuitive assumptions (as opposed to the methods of the researcher or scientist). Yet each approach has something valid to offer the other. It's like rounding off numbers to get a ballpark answer for a math problem, then double-checking for accuracy through long division.

The scientist often feels that educators bastardize and distort highly specific, careful research by turning it into a populist, self-serving jargon, and this may sometimes be the case. But just as often, scientists may be guilty of believing that they alone control the realm of research and new learning, overlooking the intelligence and resources (or benefits?) offered by other viewpoints. For example, when we think in terms of the dichotomy of the left brain and right brain, it becomes clear that traditional American education and traditional business have focused almost totally on the values of left-brained processes while discounting and overlooking those of the right brain.

Life is so complex and new insights are emerging so rapidly that thinking and communicating through metaphors and shared jargon become a shorthand or tool to keep pace; however, many subtleties get lost in these big-picture generalizations. Our concern is that we not think that we see the truth and our opponent is in error when, perhaps, we each see only one end of a very long string. To keep learning, we must keep our minds open not only to both ends of this paradox, but to unlearning what we know as new insights emerge.

Technical accuracy as to the origination of certain ways of thinking and behaviors is less important than the insight that there are opposite yet equally successful ways of processing and organizing our time and our lives. To mandate one and squelch the other is not just a 50 percent loss of possibilities, but also a loss of the synergy these two opposites can produce when they are combined.

57

'**W**hat's *that?*' Pooh interrupted.

'What's *what?*' I asked.

'What you just said—the Confusionist, Desiccated Scholar.'

'Well, let's see. The Confusionist, Desiccated Scholar is one who studies Knowledge for the sake of Knowledge, and who keeps what he learns to himself or to his own small group, writing pompous and pretentious papers that no one else can understand, rather than working for the enlightenment of others. How's that?'

'Much better,' said Pooh.

—Benjamin Hoff, *The Tao of Pooh*

left-brained thinking preference, you are probably very comfortable with conventional time management books and programs. What you may need, however, is a better understanding of the importance of play, how it links to effective time management, and how it can improve your current system. The next few chapters will also give you insight into the people you work with and your more right-brain-dominant family members.

If your score represents a heavily right-brained thinking preference, you most likely have found traditional time management rules and systems either limiting or unworkable and will welcome a more holistic process. The following chapters will provide a wealth of suggestions no matter which pattern of dominance you reflect.

If you score equally on both sets of thinking traits, you are comfortable with both types of processing and may even have developed an ability to shift when the need arises. It is important to note, however, that any profile can be improved. We can all increase our productivity, creativity, and balance by purposely increasing our ability to work in all areas of our brain.

If your answers fall to the far right or far left, look for opportunities to work with people who have the opposite profile. Another way to improve is to seek out tasks that require the opposite thinking abilities. If your answers fall in the middle area, look for opportunities to stretch your comfort in working at either end of the range.

The secret of geniuses' ac-complishments does not lie in what they have, but in how they use their brains. Geniuses such as Leonardo da Vinci, Thomas Jefferson, or Madame Curie typically had a wide range of ability. These people learned to be equally comfortable dealing with both highly structured and highly creative tasks.

Self-Assessment of Thinking Styles and Time Management Skills

Read each of the following statements and decide which describe you best. Then circle the number closest to the place you fit on the line ranging from L5 (extremely organized, plan- and routine-oriented) to R5 (extremely random, flexible, spontaneous, rarely repetitious or predictable).

If you find that you are sometimes orderly and sometimes not, you would probably fall between L3 and R3. If you find that you are extremely organized and attracted to plans and schedules at work, but just the opposite at home, *circle two numbers on the same line,* one representing work and one representing your personal life.

Let your intuition guide you as you rate yourself on each answer. Go with your first impulse.

· ·

59

1

Do you start your day by making a list, setting priorities, and sticking with them?

Do you work best by just getting started and working on several tasks at once?

L 5 .... 4 ..... 3 ..... 2 .... (1) .... 0 ..... 1 .... 2 ..... 3 .... 4 ..... 5 R

2

Is it easy for you to prioritize tasks and know how much time to allot for each?

Do you find it difficult to prioritize tasks because the order and amount of time you spend on them can change hourly based on circumstances?

L 5 .... 4 ..... 3 ..... 2 ..... 1 .... 0 .... (1) .... 2 ..... 3 .... 4 ..... 5 R

3

Do you find it easy to schedule projects and events and keep your business and social life organized with a calendar system?

Do you need to get into a project first to find out how long you need to spend on it or wait until the weekend to see if you are going to be in the mood for a social event?

L 5 .... 4 .... (3) .... (2) .... 1 .... 0 .... 1 ..... 2 ..... 3 .... 4 ..... 5 R

4

Does project follow-up come naturally for you? Do you enjoy buttoning down details?

Do you find it difficult to remember phone calls that need to be returned or questions that still need to be answered two weeks after a meeting?

L 5 .... 4 ..... 3 ..... 2 ..... 1 .... 0 ..... 1 .... (2) .... 3 .... 4 ..... 5 R

5

When planning a meeting, do you like to send out an agenda in advance so that attendees will know how to prepare and what to bring?

Do you purposely not send out an agenda to remain flexible and open to what each person and the group bring to the meeting?

L 5 .... 4 .... (3) .... 2 ..... 1 .... 0 ..... 1 ..... 2 .... 3 ..... 4 ..... 5 R

6

In meetings, do you feel more satisfied when items are brought to closure?

Do you feel best when brainstorming new ideas, working to achieve consensus, and keeping options open?

L 5 . . . . 4 . . . . . 3 . . . . . 2 . . . . 1 . . . . 0 . . . . . 1 . . . . . 2 . . . . . 3 . . . . . 4 . . . . . 5 R

7

Is it more important to you for meetings to start promptly and end on time?

Is it more important to you to be flexible, follow the group's needs, and keep going until all of the feelings and input on issues are heard and considered?

L 5 . . . . 4 . . . . . 3 . . . . . 2 . . . . 1 . . . . 0 . . . . . 1 . . . . . 2 . . . . . 3 . . . . . 4 . . . . . 5 R

8

Is your desk relatively uncluttered? Do you prefer to file things in drawers and have only one project on your desk at a time?

Do you function best when your work is within arm's reach where you can see it or stacked in piles around you?

L 5 . . . . 4 . . . . . 3 . . . . . 2 . . . . 1 . . . . . 0 . . . . . 1 . . . . . 2 . . . . 3 . . . . . 4 . . . . . 5 R

9

Do you function best when you are allowed to work on one task at a time?

Do you prefer to work on several projects at once so that you can transfer ideas from one task to another and shift back and forth to relieve fatigue?

L 5 . . . . 4 . . . . . 3 . . . . . 2 . . . . . 1 . . . . 0 . . . . . 1 . . . . . 2 . . . . 3 . . . . . 4 . . . . . 5 R

10

Do you find it easy to say no to projects that will consume too much of your time?

Do you usually say yes and then find yourself spread too thin, on too many committees, with no time left for yourself?

L 5 . . . . 4 . . . . . 3 . . . . . 2 . . . . . 1 . . . . 0 . . . . . 1 . . . . . 2 . . . . . 3 . . . . 4 . . . . . 5 R

11

If you need to communicate information to someone in another office, do you prefer to send a fax or letter to provide the recipient with a written copy?

Do you feel that people are covered up with paper and would prefer a personal phone call giving them the same information or, better yet, would you go in person when possible?

L 5 . . . . 4 . . . . 3 . . . . 2 . . . . 1 . . . . 0 . . . . 1 . . . . 2 . . . . 3 . . . . 4 . . . . 5 R

12

Are you more likely to execute a plan that has been tried and tested before, with a proven track record?

Do you enjoy initiating a fresh approach that is uniquely designed for the situation at hand? (Do the risks seem to be balanced by the benefits of innovation?)

L 5 . . . . 4 . . . . 3 . . . . 2 . . . . 1 . . . . 0 . . . . 1 . . . . 2 . . . . 3 . . . . 4 . . . . 5 R

13

When you clean your desk, a closet, or the garage, is it easy for you to throw things out?

Do you tend to get hopelessly bogged down in trivia and remain unable to throw things out?

L 5 . . . . 4 . . . . 3 . . . . 2 . . . . 1 . . . . 0 . . . . 1 . . . . 2 . . . . 3 . . . . 4 . . . . 5 R

14

Do you read books and magazines front to back, scanning the table of contents to decide which articles or chapters you want to read?

Do you frequently read magazines back to front or browse through them, or skip to the last chapter in a book to see if you want to read the middle part?

L 5 . . . . 4 . . . . 3 . . . . 2 . . . . 1 . . . . 0 . . . . 1 . . . . 2 . . . . 3 . . . . 4 . . . . 5 R

15

Are you good at estimating in advance how much time tasks will require?

Are you typically unrealistic about how much time tasks will require and stressed out with too much scheduled in too short a time?

L 5 . . . . 4 . . . . 3 . . . . 2 . . . . 1 . . . . 0 . . . . 1 . . . . 2 . . . . 3 . . . . 4 . . . . 5 R

© 1993 by Ann McGee-Cooper and Associates, Inc.

16 If you have a choice, would you rather work alone in your office on paperwork with the door shut? | Do you find yourself drawn to people, listening to them and coaching them to create solutions, with no time for the paperwork?

L 5 . . . . 4 . . . . . 3 . . . . . 2 . . . . . 1 . . . . . 0 . . . . . 1 . . . . . 2 . . . . . 3 . . . . . 4 . . . . . 5 R

---

17 If you want to put together an unassembled piece of furniture or an appliance, do you read the instructions first and follow them step-by-step? | Do you only read instructions when all else fails?

L 5 . . . . 4 . . . . . 3 . . . . . 2 . . . . . 1 . . . . 0 . . . . . 1 . . . . . 2 . . . . . 3 . . . . . 4 . . . . . 5 R

---

18 Do you like to plan things well in advance? | Do you prefer to "fly by the seat of your pants"?

L 5 . . . . 4 . . . . . 3 . . . . . 2 . . . . . 1 . . . . . 0 . . . . . 1 . . . . . 2 . . . . . 3 . . . . . 4 . . . . . 5 R

---

19 When you go grocery shopping, do you typically make a list in advance, perhaps writing items down as you run out of them? Do you group the items by their location in the store? | Do you quickly jot down a few needs and then browse through the aisles, looking for new, interesting items? Is impulse buying half the fun? Do you wait to see what fruits and vegetables are fresh or priced well?

L 5 . . . . 4 . . . . . 3 . . . . . 2 . . . . . 1 . . . . . 0 . . . . . 1 . . . . . 2 . . . . . 3 . . . . . 4 . . . . . 5 R

---

20 Is filing easy and second nature for you? Do systems and categories seem obvious? Can you locate almost everything you need because you file it when you are not working on it? | Is filing a "black hole" that frustrates and confuses you? Can you think of four titles for each folder, which are useless anyway because you usually end up with more than one file for each project?

L 5 . . . . 4 . . . . . 3 . . . . . 2 . . . . . 1 . . . . . 0 . . . . . 1 . . . . . 2 . . . . . 3 . . . . . 4 . . . . . 5 R

21 Do you almost always wear a watch?

Do you purposely look for times in your life when you can avoid wearing a watch? Is it important to you to respect your intuition and natural rhythms?

L 5 .... 4 .... 3 .... 2 .... 1 .... 0 .... 1 .... 2 .... 3 .... 4 .... 5 R

---

22 Do you pride yourself on punctuality and arrive a few minutes early to almost every appointment?

Do you often find yourself running late, pushing deadlines, and pressed for time?

L 5 .... 4 .... 3 .... 2 .... 1 .... 0 .... 1 .... 2 .... 3 .... 4 .... 5 R

---

23 Do you thrive on a predictable schedule and sequence of tasks? Do you get up, exercise, shower, dress, and eat in a regular sequence?

Do you enjoy changing your routine and surprising yourself?

L 5 .... 4 .... 3 .... 2 .... 1 .... 0 .... 1 .... 2 .... 3 .... 4 .... 5 R

---

24 Do you focus primarily on "doing" time, getting things done, and being productive?

Do you claim a balance of "being" time, time to just relax and enjoy being alive?

L 5 .... 4 .... 3 .... 2 .... 1 .... 0 .... 1 .... 2 .... 3 .... 4 .... 5 R

---

25 Do you weed out paper and belongings often and systematically, bringing things into order and eliminating the unnecessary?

Do you wish order would magically appear? Does your fun come from starting projects, not from cleaning up, bringing order, or throwing out the trivia?

L 5 .... 4 .... 3 .... 2 .... 1 .... 0 .... 1 .... 2 .... 3 .... 4 .... 5 R

Charting Your Profile

After you have answered each question, look for the general pattern of your answers. Do more of them fall to the left or the right? Or do they often fall in the middle range?

Beginning with the first page, make a cumulative total of all the numbers you circled to the left of the "0" on the scoring line. After you calculate this number, label it your L-Score. Next, add up all the numbers you circled to the right of the "0." After you determine this number, label it your R-Score. We have designated thinking traits generally associated with left-hemisphere function as L-Score and traits generally associated with right-hemisphere function as R-Score. These two scores represent how much of your thinking is influenced by your right- and left-brained thinking traits.

Remember, neither thinking style is better. Both sets of traits are valuable and important in different ways.

We will show you how you can use these new insights into your own working and thinking preferences to improve your time management and your teaming with opposite styles and, in general, to create a far more rewarding life-style.

But before we explore specific right-brained enhancers for traditional left-brained time management systems, let's take a second look at some traditional time management advice that needs to be revised for right-brained folks.

"WHAT'S GOOD for GENERAL BULLMOOSE is good for the U.S.A..!"

66 If you obey all the rules you miss all the fun. **99**

—Katharine Hepburn

66 As time passes we all get better at blazing a trail through the thicket of advice. **99**

—Margot Bennett

66 Selfishness is not living as one wishes to live, it is asking others to live as one wishes to live. **99**

—Oscar Wilde

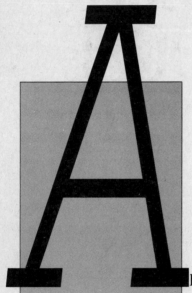l Capp, the well-known cartoonist who created "Li'l Abner," also created a character named General Bullmoose. Described as a "venial and corrupt capitalist," General Bullmoose had the philosophy that "progress is the root of all evil." He would make all the rules and it was everyone else's job to follow them,

as he proclaimed, "What's good for General Bullmoose is good for the U.S.A.!"

Unfortunately, this is what has happened with much of the advice on time management. Because it works for the people giving the advice, they assume it must be good for everyone. But unless you share their tendencies, processing patterns, and ways of learning, it may cripple and limit you far more than it helps you. Let us see why this is true.

There's a good chance that if you purchased this book, the right-brained questions on the self-assessment in the preceding chapter pegged you. It might have even been a bit spooky to realize how closely we described some of your working and thinking habits. Chances are, too, that somewhere down the line you've said to yourself, "I just can't seem to get organized. There's got to be an answer to this." You may have gone to the bookstore and bought a book about time management or, better yet, signed up for a seminar or an intensive crash course.

If you read a traditional time management book or attended a traditional time management course, you were probably given a lecture about your nasty, disorganized bad habits and pre-

sented with a list of Time Management Commandments. You were grateful for the opportunity to confess your time management sins, redeem yourself, and start once again on the road to salvation. As you left the seminar, you vowed to never again fall prey to your bad habits. But, alas, in less than two hours, you were back to writing notes on little pieces of paper, keeping files out where you could find them, and working on six things at once. And now you had the added guilt of knowing that you had transgressed.

BAD HABITS MAY BE GOOD HABITS IN DISGUISE

Did it ever occur to you that what they told you in those books and seminars might be right for them, but not right for you? In fact, those "bad habits" that they wanted you to get rid of might be giftedness you were simply wearing wrong-side-out. Perhaps your way of doing things (with a little adjustment) could work just as effectively for you as their way does for them.

Let's look at a few typical time management rules, the implied "bad habits" that are a part of them, and the fallacies they are built on.

"A Messy Desk Is the Sign of a Cluttered Mind"

A messy desk is one problem that plagues a good many folks. Would it surprise you to learn that if you routinely work in an apparent sea of confusion, you are probably a visual processor? The mess is a problem only if you can't find most things when you need them. "If you can find most things in three minutes or less, your system is working. Don't change it," says Dr. Dru Scott, author of *How to Put More Time in Your Life*. A messy desk is the sign of a messy desk—no more, no less. It is not a reflection on your intellect, talent, or ancestry!

You know better than anyone else if your system is out of control. If you aren't able to locate what you need, if you forget commitments and miss deadlines, if you can't find all the information that you have been given, then you have a problem. But what if your work space is covered with files and papers, and it works for you? Isn't that what a work space is supposed to provide—space for your work?

"Don't Put It Down Until You File It"

In terms of Brain Engineering, this may be happening: if you are vis-
ual, you remember things and locate them visually, not abstractly. You remember them by what they look like, particularly what they look like in relation to other things; you can see Project X in your mind on the corner of your desk under the glue bottle. The surest way to forget something or lose it completely is to file it. All files look more or less the same. They become black holes into which things vanish. You know a paper was filed because you remember filing it, but you can't for the life of you remember where or how—it has disappeared. Or you may have four files for the same project but can't find any of them so you start a fifth file, only this time you leave it on the corner of your desk so you can find it.

I am a visual person, so I am speaking from years of frustration. My other problem is that I am very divergent. The reason I can't find a file is not because I don't know the alphabet but because I see too many options. If I were to file the manuscript for this book, I might put it under "T" for time, "M" for

manuscript, "N" for new book, or "W" for writing project. Then, when I need it, I might look under "P" for publishing project.

If you are a convergent thinker, this will sound ridiculous to you, and I can assure you that it feels ridiculous to me when I spend hours looking for a piece of paper I know I filed. My solution is to leave it in plain sight, but with so many projects going on simultaneously, a lot of folders are "in plain sight." The result is a messy desk.

Typically, if you are a visual person, you are also a spatial person. You put things down in spaces that make sense to you. The folders by my phone are those relating to pending phone calls. The folders on the top right corner of my desk are related to the budgeting projects that will be going on during the next three months. Those on the southwest corner are related to Comanche Peak, because that project is southwest of here. I remember how to find things by relating them to locations.

I have found that I can go into top management's offices and "read" their "piling" system. After they have produced their ritual apology for a messy desk, I ask if I might describe their system to them. It usually takes only a few minutes to discover the logic to their visual placement of stacks and folders. After I describe it to them, they recognize for the first time that it really isn't a hopeless mess made by a slob who just can't get his or her act together, but the carefully orchestrated system of a right-brained person who remembers and functions from visual and spatial clues. Instead of kicking yourself or expecting to accomplish your work in a left-brained, abstract way, why not accept your differences and learn to enjoy and appreciate the gifts and values of the unique ways your brain works?

There are other interesting subconscious reasons for leaving stacks and folders visible in your work space. If you are a divergent person, you probably do your best work when you are juggling several projects simultaneously. When you become blocked or tired of one project, you shift to another. You frequently come up with great ideas about a project you have tabled while you're off on another task.

There are two other reasons why it helps me to leave work in plain sight:

1. I remember to get back to the task in a timely manner.

2. I'm subconsciously reminded to incubate. Then, when it's time for me to produce, I have

thought enough about the project to have collected a number of good insights and creative options.

You can see that tidiness for a right-brained person is a waste of time. As you begin to work on getting rid of the rule that your desk must be neat to be efficient, consider ignoring some other traditional time management rules that don't fit a divergent style.

"Finish One Task Before Beginning Another"

If you insist on working on one task at a time, you may quickly get burned out. This results in less and less quality in more and more time. Does it really make sense for you to compulsively push yourself to complete a task when instead you might shift gears, refresh yourself, and then come back to finish it?

In a previous book, *You Don't Have to Go Home from Work Exhausted!* we encouraged the use of joy breaks to interrupt the pressure of routine and improve productivity. Another strategy is to work on several tasks simultaneously, learning from one what you need to complete the others.

For example, in our office we often block out two or three seminars or draft several articles at

once. We have learned to take each as far as we can, then give it to an editor, colleague, or partner to edit, critique, and add to. By passing an article back and forth, we find that we easily get a significantly improved result in less time with far less effort. And none of us suffer from the paper barrier that we used to confront on a regular basis.

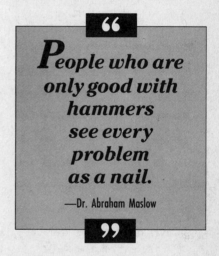

> ## *People who are only good with hammers see every problem as a nail.*
> —Dr. Abraham Maslow

The test is to trust your partners to see and improve your less-than-perfect first attempt. This takes courage at first, but as the trust builds, you will probably be surprised at what you learn. We have learned that we often can dash out an 80 percent draft that can easily be polished by a partner. And all this can happen in half the time and effort we used to spend, individually and as a team,

Organizing Your Desk

Getting Started

Go to an office supply or container store and collect visual aids to organization. (We will discuss this at length in Chapter Eight.) Buy colored file folders, clear Lucite boxes and containers, baskets in all sizes, brightly colored file cabinets, and any other storage units that appeal to you. Keep your eyes open at antique shops and flea markets for containers you like. They don't have to be official "office" supplies.

I remember where things are by their color, texture, location, and other unique visual properties. I like to keep each current project in its own basket with handles. Then I can move all the information to a big table, spread it out, and work on it. I can also take it outside to a picnic table, to my partner Duane's office, to my executive assistant Linda's office, or to the lake for a weekend work session between naps, painting, and golf.

Clients in large corporations have adapted this system by using large sweater boxes for big projects such as audits, legal cases, engineering projects, or proposals. Then all the materials can be kept together and moved all at once. Often just moving to a fresh location helps us to get a new perspective on a project.

when each of us was attempting to be perfect the first time without help.

Another benefit is that most of our projects blend our talents more than they did in the past. Formerly, we each felt responsible for "carrying" our share of the work. Without ever discussing it, we did our work to the very best of our ability, *then* asked others to review it, if at all. With the current system, much more gets done with a lot more energy, satisfaction, and ease. Most of the struggle is gone. We have found that when we do find ourselves dragging our heels, procrastinating, or dreading a task, talking through our fears and anxieties with another partner usually helps us get past the mental blocks. If we held fast to the "finish one task" rule, we'd probably be stuck forever.

As you can see, the traditional rule makes sense to a convergent thinker but blocks, frustrates, and needlessly sabotages a divergent thinker. By learning to trust and honor your inner signals, you will find that you will produce far more work of much higher quality.

"Handle Each Piece of Paper Only Once"

This is a classic time management rule; it encourages you to take action in the moment rather than returning twice to the same spot. This rule came into popularity when bureaucracies flourished and it was possible to put one's stamp on a paper and pass it to a higher or lower level for action. But anyone who works in an office in which decisions require input or approval from several sources can't "handle each piece of paper only once." Often, it is necessary to gather from others the information, commitments, or reactions needed to take action or answer questions about the original "piece of paper." There is a balancing value in "paper shuffling" that most people overlook. Sometimes you aren't ready to answer a letter because you don't know enough about the situation. By quickly glancing at the letter, you remind your brain to incubate and get ready to write or to keep searching until you come up with the best response.

In a more technical sense, handling each piece of paper only once denies the power of the subconscious. The first reading of a document establishes a position for it in both your conscious and subconscious minds. Revisiting stimulates both, but the subconscious has been working on the problem all along. If you answer the issue immediately, you limit

For some people, clutter sends a message of junk and unfinished business. For others of us it is like an old and trusted friend who comforts us.

your brainpower to only your immediate, conscious thoughts.

As I quickly sift through my stacks, I remind myself of what is waiting and what needs my attention or creative imagination. Sometimes I do find myself juggling paper just to keep from getting on with business, but I know when I'm doing that. Instead of always following the same pattern, bending the rules so that they serve you (rather than you slavishly serving them) saves time and allows for more creativity and joy at work and at home.

"Plan Well in Advance and Stick to Your Plan"

It is true that this gives us the advantage of ample lead time, which is an advantage I always used to lose by letting my work slide until the last minute. However, a balancing option is to constantly review and challenge your plan. There is so much change in our business and personal lives that what made great sense last week may be obsolete now. For example, last week I had an executive assistant and an editor available. This week one is out with a critically ill family member and the other has double pneumonia. How can we make our plans flexible

A Word About Kitchens

Kitchens are interesting places. Some cooks put everything behind doors "so they can find them." They have a logical, abstract system for locating what they need. Other cooks have to leave everything out in order to locate what they have. I am one of those cooks. I like my pans on a rack on the wall, my utensils in an earthenware jar by the stove, and trays and baskets overhead. Under the cabinets are big, open, wire mesh baskets filled with bowls, jars, and other supplies. I can easily spot what I need without opening every door in the kitchen.

If you are a convergent, abstract organizer, all this may look like clutter to you and tire you in a hurry. The environment that gives visual people the energy to enjoy cooking and being in the kitchen drains your enthusiasm. You crave a clean, uncluttered space for your work; what feels empty and barren to me would seem delightfully organized and inviting to you.

It is essential for us to understand our opposites and talk about ways to create a good working compromise that will be satisfying to both points of view. The same principles are at work in the office as in the kitchen. Look at the desks of your co-workers. Talking about work styles and how people organize things will help you work more effectively with your opposites.

enough to meet all our commitments without abusing the health or limits of any one person?

We frequently find that some of our most successful and creative breakthroughs for increased productivity happen when such unplanned emergencies occur. When we discover an untapped ability because of a crisis, we are eager to keep growing in this new skill area. By combining advanced planning with staying flexible, spontaneous, and open to change, you can create a whole-brained balance in yourself.

"Get Rid of What You Don't Need or Use"

Do you suffer because your home, office, garage, files, and closets are pregnant with outdated stuff you can't toss out? We divergent people are masters at thinking of sixty-eight reasons why we might need these things someday—but we really need only one reason: We may become famous and our elementary school art may become a collectors' item. Meanwhile our organization gets hopelessly lost in the magnitude of our archives and in the random-access filing system we have created.

I'll admit that there certainly is a downside and a price to pay for this right-brained, not-in-vogue work style. But there are also many benefits to this approach. For example, I often discover lost ideas, concepts, treasures, and projects that I had long since forgotten as I dig through a file cabinet searching for something else. These resurrected "treasures" sometimes spark an idea or are just what I need for a current project.

One of the things we love about the Smithsonian Institution or grandma's attic is their offering of forgotten treasures. As we look back, we rediscover our roots emotionally and intellectually and connect our fragmented past with the current moment. Staying in touch with our past is a significant part of creating quality and deep joy in our lives along with highly efficient productivity.

Think of all the objects you take along with you in this fast-changing world as reminders of your roots. Or maybe it's your nest of fertile memories and past associations that nurtures and renews you. For some people, clutter sends a message of junk and unfinished business. For others of us it is like an old and trusted friend who comforts us. These echoes of our past are potential triggers for new ideas and possibilities.

Get Curious About What You Typically "Don't Have Time For"

Some time ago, my partner, Duane, and I were observing our current dilemma of time problems. I was noting that I just never seem to have time for the filing, details, putting things away, and planning that he is so good at. And he laughed, confessing that he just doesn't know where I find time for the telephone calls, meetings, and creative brainstorming that I enjoy so much. Suddenly a light dawned for us both. We realized that we devote the majority of our time to the tasks we enjoy and that seem to pay off for us and then "run out of time" for tasks we struggle with.

We knew that learning to devote a small amount of time each day to opposite-dominance tasks could bring an enormous new energy and synergy to our productivity. We began to positively encourage and coach each other on ways to approach this balance. This led us to another fascinating insight. Duane now encourages me to go long on my gifts and not worry so much about the structure and details that sap my energy and enthusiasm. And in the same way, I encourage him to focus on his strengths. We each get the greatest payoff from our strengths.

However, if you don't have a good balancing partner, you may find that you are sabotaging yourself by only focusing on your long suit of talents. Without Duane or others on our team who are gifted with structure, I would soon be lost in the chaos of my divergent nature. And Duane confesses that if others didn't stop him and question whether there might not be a new, more creative approach, he might stay entrenched in obsolete processes.

The answers are not clear-cut, but it helps both of us to know that whenever we say we don't have time for something, it is typically because we have subconsciously set ourselves up to run out of time doing the things we enjoy and trust most. We now know that we can change our focus whenever we need or want to. This insight has given us a tremendous new freedom in the way we use time.

Of course, the best solution is probably a compromise. I am embarrassed to admit that when I become overwhelmed with all my stuff, I typically get busy culling the belongings of other family members. Mine are all treasures! I do the same at work. It's usually other people's junk and clutter that bothers me. Mine always seems to have purpose and reason. But I do want to keep the goodwill and cooperation of my family and work partners, so I have found it important to clean out and let go of my treasures every now and then. And after the fact, I usually rejoice.

why TRADITIONAL Time Management doesn't WORK FOR SOME OF US

7

> **"** I refuse to be intimidated by reality anymore. After all, what is reality anyway? Nothin' but a collective hunch. My space chums think reality was once a primitive method of crowd control that got out of hand. In my view, it's absurdity dressed up in a three-piece business suit. **"**
>
> —Jane Wagner, *The Search for Signs of Intelligent Life in the Universe* (as performed by Lily Tomlin in her one-woman show)

> **"** Life consists not in holding good cards but in playing those you do hold well. **"**
>
> —Josh Billings

ost traditional time

management systems include four basic

steps: (1) plan, (2) prioritize, (3) schedule,

and (4) follow your plan. While these sys-

tems work perfectly well for some people,

they have serious flaws for many others.

First, let's look at some of those flaws.

Flow 1

Traditional time management systems have been designed primarily by left-brain-dominant people. The problem is that these rules just aren't "user-friendly" for right-brain-dominant people, who account for about half the population.

Phlaw 2

Traditional time management focuses primarily on increasing productivity and efficiency, but it ignores the needs and habits that foster innovation, adaptability, and creativity. If you only use traditional techniques, it's very possible that you may become more efficient at the same time that you become less innovative. You may be incredibly efficient at doing things in outmoded ways!

Flaugh 3

Traditional time management encourages thinking and planning in monochronic time, while ig-

noring the many benefits of becoming skillful in the use of polychronic time. Futurists predict an increasing need for intuitive leadership, interdependent teaming, advanced people skills, and the ability to innovate, based on a blend of monochronic and polychronic skills.

Flau 4

Traditional time management typically ignores the need for recreation and playtime, viewing time spent daydreaming or socializing as wasted, unfocused, and inefficient. If your entire emphasis is on getting your work done and you just give your personal fun and family time what is left over, you'll be too tired when you finally get home and have time to play. And if you limit your time management strategies to using only half your brain, you will become a prime candidate for burnout.

Pflaw 5

Traditional time management focuses on convergent skill building, measured by tangible objectives. While these are important, they are only half the process. Unless you learn to slow down and suspend and reverse time, you will throw your body into hurry sickness, threaten your physical health, and atrophy vital potential within your brain.

---

fflaw 6

Traditional time management assumes that everything can be solved and dealt with at the logical, conscious level. Yet the quantum leaps of breakthrough thinking or other significant intuitive knowledge are illogical and nonlinear. If our total approach and system of rewards is focused on linear, logical, sequential, tangible data, we have limited ourselves to the past and cannot expand into the future.

> **" *Minds that don't change are like clams that don't open.* "**
>
> Ursula LeGuin
> *Dancing at the Edge of the World*

As you can see, there are major gaps in traditional time management systems. Although they appear to work well for most strongly left-brain-dominant people, many of us either are right-brain-dominant or regularly use both sides of the brain. In order to stay healthy, creative, and productive, we need to balance our time management system to include the needs of both the left and right brain—work and play, productivity and innovation, and monochronic and polychronic thinking.

Let's look more closely at why these four perfectly logical steps work so successfully for convergent, left-brained thinkers and yet sabotage divergent, right-brained thinkers.

PLAN

"Let's See, What Could I Do Today? Making a List Is Fun!"

The usual way to begin to manage your time is by making a "to-do" list. Even in this apparently simple task, there are great differences between people with right and left brain dominance. The left brain asks, "What *should* be done today?" while the right

" Opposing Views

A and B are standing on opposite sides of a curved wall.

From A's point of view the wall is convex, while from B's viewpoint the wall is concave.

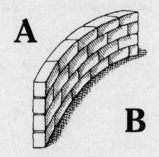

From our viewpoint, we can see the wall is both concave and convex.

Similarly, when examining a problem or an issue, we should take care to look at it from as many points of view as possible, hoping to gain a more complete view.

—Jim Young, *A Box of Pearls*

"

For those of us who are divergent thinkers, however, making a to-do list gets more complicated. Even though we are at work, we don't feel inclined to list only work-related chores. As we begin making our lists, we might think of supplies to be picked up for gardening, tennis, or other hobbies. We then might write down a few items related to the work waiting on the desk. Next, our minds shift and we begin brainstorming, coming up with totally new ideas that really get our juices flowing. Oh, yes, there are those personal letters and thank-you's we need to write. What about theater or basketball tickets for next season? Our list becomes a divergent collection of everything that pops into our heads. It isn't logical or practical, necessarily; it's just what comes to mind in the process of listing things we need to do or want to do.

By the time the list is finished, we have come up with several new and inviting ideas. We are much more attracted to new projects than to finishing old, existing ones. With all good intentions of starting a list of items that need our immediate attention, we end up with great ideas that send us off in totally different, exciting directions. (Our left-brain-dominant counterparts

brain asks, "What *could* be done today?" For those people who think convergently, list making is simple. They automatically screen out everything except the tasks at hand that need to be put on the list. And if they are at work, they typically limit their list to work demands.

"No List Is Going to Be Boss of Me!"

There may be a touch of rebelliousness involved in your list making. A friend and her husband go through the process of outlining what they need to get done each week and make a day-by-day schedule. Although they are both basically right-brained, she has developed more of her left brain than he has. So she does her chores pretty much as they decide during the planning session, but he does his Thursday chores on Tuesday, his Tuesday chores on Wednesday—and some of the Friday chores are still waiting. He gets a charge out of doing them that way—as if he were somehow victorious over the onerous list—even through he participated in making it. It seems as if there is something about the list that some of us rebel against as if another person were dictating it to us.

---

call them tangents.) The process of making the to-do list actually turns into a brainstorming session that assures us that we're too busy to finish up old, less interesting projects. Another problem is that the list becomes so long that it is intimidating. We look at the thirty-five or so items before us as a wonderful smorgasbord of choices, so we sample and taste up and down the entire list rather than expecting to complete everything we start.

At the end of this first step in traditional time management—the planning step—the convergent person has a nice, tidy, doable list of responsibilities for the day or week, while the divergent person has just dreamed up all sorts of new dragons to be slain and has no better idea how to get the things done that still need doing than when the list was started. It could easily take six people to complete my typical Monday morning to-do list, and the lists from last Friday, and Thursday, and all the other days have items still waiting to be completed. In fact, I have a stack of to-do lists. Just take your pick.

I suspect that one of the reasons we divergent people frequently misplace our to-do lists is that they are such an overwhelming reminder of the abundance of our imagination. They serve to make us feel hopelessly behind, because we can't see how we can ever catch up and get all those things done. Especially if we are making new lists every day!

PRIORITIZE

"If It Weren't a Priority, I Wouldn't Have Listed It in the First Place."

The next step in traditional time management appears obvious and practical for the convergent thinker. We are instructed to put the items on the list in order of priority by dividing the list into three groups: "A" for most important, "B" for next in importance, and "C" for least important. Again, the reason this system works so well for the left brain and not at all for the right lies in the different way each hemisphere understands and processes this "simple" task.

First of all, the divergent brain rarely stays in one place long enough to agree on a priority. Although an item may be very important now, it may not be quite as important after I have talked with a new client on the phone. Suddenly, the priorities have changed and the new client is now more important. Second, whereas the left brain has the gift of clearly thinking in terms of black and white, the right-brained thinker sees an infinite number of shades of gray. Think of the left brain as operating much like a light switch. It's either on or off. A task is either important or not.

The distinction is clear-cut. But the right-brained process is more like a dimmer switch with an infinite range of levels. Instead of quickly coming up with A, B, or C, we come up with something more like A, a, A+, A++, Ab++, B++, or "really more important than B but less important than A."

There is also a tendency for right-brained people not to list less important items in the first place. Everything on the list seems really important or it just isn't there. For example, while paperwork must be done, it probably won't be on the list because it isn't interesting or exciting or perceived of as important. It's just a boring task that "somebody" will take care of "sometime."

Even the process of trying to prioritize the list wears us out!

SCHEDULE

"Calendars Just Don't Work for Me!"

This step sounds relatively easy; just go to an office supply store and pick out a calendar. But do I want a "Day-at-a-Glance," a "Week-at-a-Glance," or a "Month-at-a-Glance"? Do I want a pocket-sized, desk-sized, or wall calendar? Maybe I need one of those new programs that puts your schedule on the computer.

87

We who are divergent are likely to want to think about the decision a little longer or to keep researching the possibilities (divergent types typically want to keep all their options open!). Or, even more deadly, we may buy one of each type to see which works best. If we buy a small one to carry and a large one for the wall, we are apt to forget to move appointments from the small calendar to the large one. Or we make notes on scraps of paper since the pocket calendar is home on the dresser; then we misplace the notes and double-schedule ourselves, or we miss the appointment. Soon we are heard lamenting, "Calendars just don't work for me!"

FOLLOW YOUR PLAN

"Now, What Was I Supposed to Do?"

The fourth step to traditional time management seems to be the most troublesome for us divergent folks, yet it is the easiest for convergent people. Once the plan is carefully crafted, following through is the fun and payoff for the left-brained and convergent thinker. We divergent, right-brained thinkers, on the other hand, are bored and weary once we have gotten this far. We crave fresh ideas, fresh challenges, and fresh directions. I suspect that my own tendency to be too busy for daily planning meetings and to constantly misplace my calendar or to-do list has a lot to do with my wish for something totally new.

Another problem for us is that we are responsive to people. Many times, interruptions are a welcome break from the boring drudgery of "the plan." And what if we just aren't in the mood to write a new article for the company newsletter, even though the calendar says it's what we're supposed to be doing? Our need for spontaneity, flexibility, and fresh opportunities makes it easy for us to miss out on the seemingly obvious benefits of sticking with the plan. The more detailed, rigid, and repetitious the plan, the more difficult it will be for a divergent person to stick to it. While the convergent personality welcomes the life-style of planned predictability, the divergent personality often finds the routine stifling and somewhat claustrophobic.

This is not to say that a plan and a creative planning process can't become a tremendous as-set for the right-brained, divergent person. But unless or until we understand how to tailor this part of the process to the unique needs and gifts of a diverger, we may find ourselves constantly frustrated by what may seem to be our obstinate lack of follow-through.

That's the bad news. The good news is that a multitude of creative strategies exist to keep us focused on our goals. The next chapters will reveal tips and insights that will help you to understand your own special needs and show you how to plan so that you work *with,* not *against,* your strengths and special gifts. Another tremendous benefit is the new appreciation and understanding you will gain for all the many ways you might lose your focus; you will learn how to harness unfocused energies until they become a part of your natural momentum. And if you are a naturally convergent person, you'll gain many insights to expand both your understanding of others and your toolbox of strategies, enabling you to team and produce far more effectively, with more energy, fun, and satisfaction. Judging, blaming, and coercing others only wastes time and drains vital energy.

8

PLANNING:
How to Limit
Your TO-DO LIST
to THREE HUNDRED ITEMS

> **"** Our two greatest problems are gravity and paper work. We can lick gravity, but sometimes the paper work is overwhelming. **"**
>
> —Dr. Wernher von Braun

> **"** I didn't bite off more than I could chew—it just grew in my mouth. **"**
>
> —Dr. Robert Ballard
> on his search for the *Titanic*

> **"** We can keep busy rearranging the deck chairs on the sinking *Titanic*, but this ignores the obvious problem. **"**
>
> —Dr. Eric Allenbaugh
> *Wake-Up Calls*

DO MORE
DO IT NOW
DO THE
IMPOSSIB
DO YC

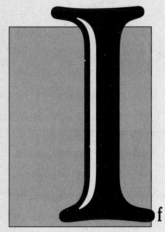

f you find that you typically frustrate yourself with unrealistic lists and as a result you rarely have the satisfaction of marking off every item, consider a few tips that can help make the process fun and manageable.

First, change your basic expectations. If you always accomplish everything on your list, you are working from uncreative planning.

A basic assumption in brainstorming is that you generate a wealth of possibilities and then narrow the list to those with the most potential. If you don't realize this, you may go for the easier or more doable tasks because you are not sure how to tackle the more demanding but promising or fertile opportunities. The Swiss-cheese approach (breaking an overwhelming task into smaller tasks) will work for this problem. But even knowing not to expect to accomplish everything you think up can be very important. Just go for the really great ideas.

BUY FUN NEW ORGANIZING SUPPLIES

The next step is to visit an office supply store and search for some interesting props to motivate your playful side and make it fun to write a to-do list. Buy different-colored Post-it™ Notes, silly pens, colored clips, unusual notepads, and fluorescent file folders. If this sounds too frivolous, limit your purchases on this first trip to twenty dollars.

For a convergent thinker, this would be a big waste of time and money. If you have manila file folders, conventional paper clips, standard clasp envelopes, and legal pads, why buy new stuff?

However, isn't it worth twenty dollars a month to stay organized? For me, these colored markers, tablets, and Post-its are just as essential to my well-being as a balanced breakfast. They provide the momentum to keep me focused and motivated.

You should also know that for the divergent thinker, any system only works for a while. We soon tire of a system and want a change just for the sake of variety. Plan a monthly shopping trip to the office supply store to look for new, interesting supplies. You may not know how you are going to use them at first, but buy them anyway. If they appeal to you, you'll figure out why you need them after you get home or to your office. If it helps, think of these goodies as your reward for staying organized and bringing more balance and creativity into your life.

MAKE A LIST, KEEP IT MANAGEABLE, AND REWARD YOURSELF

When you are ready to make your to-do list, choose a few of your colorful new supplies and write your list in your usual manner. We suggest placing each item on a small Post-it Note so that you can move the notes around and don't have to spend

Collect Memorable Idea Catchers!

Several years ago, I was collecting all my to-do list pads and notebooks to take to a seminar as examples of how much fun it can be to keep lists going if you allow yourself to buy colorful, appealing, and even outrageous supplies. Once I got them all together, I was amazed at their number and variety. Then I began to realize that, like a small child, I tire of my supplies over time and crave new ones to keep my work process fun.

I now know that the enjoyment in using new supplies provides the balance I need to keep me on track. This rich variety of lively and memorable "idea catchers" has another hidden benefit. I can easily remember where I wrote something down by the color and uniqueness of the pad. Now you might think that no self-respecting engineer, accountant, or lawyer would be caught dead with a collection of crazy notepads or comic to-do pads, but we have been surprised and delighted at how creative and energized our clients become when they give themselves permission to add these items to their work.

One funny discovery was a pad three inches thick that opened at either end. During the seminar I found that, in my typical divergent pattern, I had lists going at either end of this pad. So I simply converted this mistake into an asset. I now keep my personal and family to-do's at one end and business to-do's at the other. Get curious about how your brain works and have fun making use of your unique assets and patterns.

so much time copying them over from list to list. *After your grand list is compiled, find another sheet and move onto it only the tasks that are most important and that you are sure you can complete before noon.* Using Post-it Notes will appeal to your right brain; it will feel as if you are playing a board game as you move them around. To make it even more interesting, use different-colored notes and ink for your list.

Draw a line below the items you have collected and add something to reward yourself with when you complete all the items by noon. Be sure to make the reward something that's fun and worth wish-

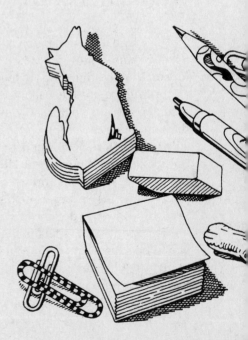

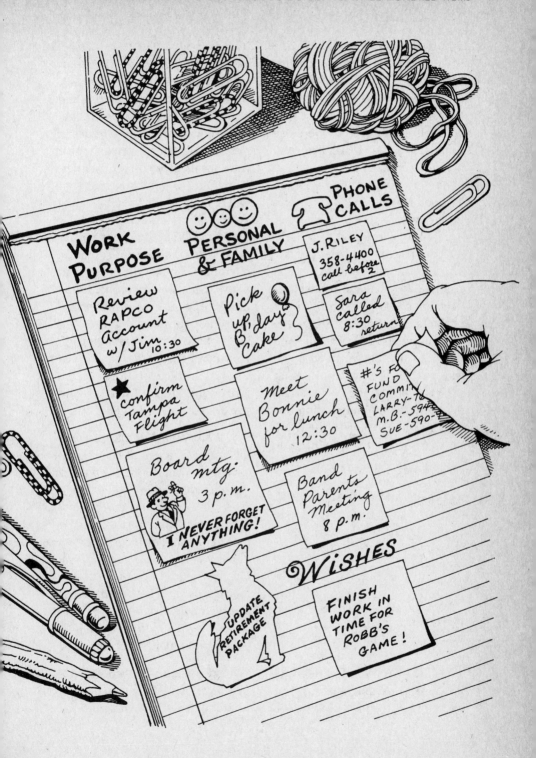

ing for. It might be a special lunch break—a picnic in the park with a friend, a trip to a new restaurant, or a browse through a downtown bookstore. Go ahead and reward yourself if you even come close to finishing your tasks. The goal here is to unlearn nonproductive habits, so congratulate yourself for good work even if it isn't quite perfect yet.

Below where you have written your reward, you may put any other items you wish to accomplish today, but make a conscious decision not to start any of these projects until you have done the ones above the line and collected your reward. Set yourself up to win. Part of the problem is that for your entire life, your abundant and fertile imagination has set you up to lose with the traditional to-do list. Even if you came close to meeting the ambitious goals set out on your list, you felt an urge to add more things to it. (I'm speaking from experience again. There are *always* more ideas to add to the list!)

IS FUN ON YOUR LIST?

If we try to follow traditional time management rules, we strive hard to put only work items on our list of things to do. Forget that rule! If we limit ourselves to work ideas, it is no surprise that we lose interest and momentum as the day wears on.

We will discuss joy breaks in detail in Chapter Twelve, but for now, let us give you a quick version. A joy break is anything that will rest and renew you by taking your mind off work for a little while. Call your significant other and make a date for a romantic evening or weekend. Stop to read a few "Far Side" cartoons. Enjoy an apple or put on a tape of music you enjoy for a few minutes.

Bobbie Little, managing director of the Raleigh, North Carolina, office of Drake Beam Morin, Inc., tells of her favorite joy break:

"I buy funny, attractive cards wherever I happen to be (the airport, the grocery store, the mall). I keep a supply in my office. When it's Stress Central in my office, I will take a ten-minute break to write a funny comment or a quick note to a friend, colleague, or family member with whom I need to stay in touch. This way I get a break, cross something off my list, and feel creative! I return to work feeling guilty, wicked, and totally recharged!"

Try seeing what would happen if you actually wrote down a reminder to take a morning joy break. Use it to plan lunch. Think of some way to make lunchtime special, enjoyable, and renewing. Maybe you can browse through a shop you enjoy or take a turn through a museum and eat in the tearoom. Why not walk down to your local Farmers' Market and have lunch at an outdoor café with a friend?

Or you might use the time to plan your evening fun when work is finished. By doing this when you are refreshed, you not only free the best of your creative imagination; you also have the energy to think up good ideas and the time to prepare thoroughly. For example, you can plan a dinner out with friends, call the friends, make reservations at the restaurant—and voilà, your evening is ready to enjoy. As an added bonus, you have the whole rest of the day to enjoy looking forward to a pleasant evening.

We have learned that the very act of anticipating something we enjoy changes the chemistry in our brains and gives us wonderful benefits that build energy, counter stress, and enhance our teaming and creativity skills. So don't limit your list to work tasks. Balance the work items with play items and watch the results. You can expect to get more done, at higher quality, in less time with

more time left for fun. Try it and decide for yourself!

KEEP YOUR SELF-TALK POSITIVE

Begin with baby steps, and give yourself several weeks to fine-tune the process so that you get to win every day and celebrate your balance of fun and work. This technique helped me to control my inclination toward the "superwoman syndrome" and allowed me to gain a much healthier perspective and balance to my life. It has also worked for

We have learned that the very act of anticipating something we enjoy changes the chemistry in our brains and gives us wonderful benefits.

hundreds of other people. Just remember not to be afraid to take some poetic license with the process.

Think of yourself as a Brain Engineer, the one designing the process. Play with your tendencies, your likes and dislikes. Develop respect for areas you don't like or find difficult to stick with. Become curious about why you are as you are. You are a fascinating, complex, and unique blending of right- and left-brained tendencies. Take the time to play with strategies that allow you to use your patterns and strengths in positive ways.

Keep in mind, however, that balance comes slowly and is most

Head and Shoulders Above the Clutter

One of my favorite props to keep me on track is a clear, legal-sized Lucite clipboard that stands up on a base. I put my Post-it Notes of to-do's on that stand and move it with me all day long. It stands above the clutter, so it isn't likely to get lost or buried. And it appeals to my playful visual side.

Spatial placement on the clipboard is important. The most important tasks get moved to the top left corner while the least important tasks move to the bottom right. It is energizing to be able to shift priorities and easily move everything into a new position, creating a game that is whole-brained fun for me and for our team. When I tire of the clipboard, I put my notes on a colored legal pad or across the front of a fancy leather notebook. The most important concept is to keep the process fun and inviting.

Another helpful organizing tip involves finding a way to capture ideas for the many parts of your life. Make your notes as you think of them—not, as we have seen, a necessarily orderly process—then group like ideas together in columns on your clipboard or notebook. In addition to business ideas, I keep a column for my gardening ideas, one for my social life, and one for building projects. When I run out of space on the clipboard, I use colored notepads to collect ideas. With Post-its, I can easily add and discard ideas.

likely to emerge if we are gentle, appreciative, nurturing, and encouraging with ourselves as well as with others. You are probably much gentler with the mistakes and bad habits of others than you are with your own. Rather than fighting change or blaming yourself for not getting it all right at once, be forgiving and supportive of yourself.

I used to get discouraged and embarrassed because I seemed to be forever setting up new systems, instead of following up on the old ones. I heaped guilt and punishment on myself, vowing: "No more new notebooks until you demonstrate that you can stick to a system!" (Can you hear the convergent logic in this?) Then I realized that my goal was to keep myself organized, not tie myself to a system. If that meant a new system each week, so be it. In reality, I find that I am in the good company of about half the population, who typically rotate from system to system. We also borrow systems from each other to constantly improve the basic process.

If you insist on blaming yourself, feeling like a failure, and thinking that you are inferior to "organized" people, you will trigger a defensive response that will rob you of energy and make you less open and honest with yourself and with others. Then, instead of devising a process that can work for you, you will spend your time making excuses, feeling guilty, and being generally bummed out. Learn instead to be gentle, curious, and patient.

Eliminate your guilt and begin discovering stimulating ways to get organized. The process is fun and a challenge, one you will be good at very soon.

> ## *Don't put off for tomorrow what you can do today, because if you enjoy it today you can do it again tomorrow.*
>
> —James A. Michener

PRIORITIZING:
A MILLION
Changing
SHADES *of* GRAY

9

66 Whenever you set out to do something, something else must be done first. **99**

—Murphy's Law, Corollary 6

66 Which brings us back to Owl. Let's see—how did Rabbit describe the situation with Owl? Oh, here it is:

> ... you can't help respecting anybody who can spell TUESDAY, even if he doesn't spell it right; but spelling isn't everything. There are days when spelling Tuesday simply doesn't count. **99**

—Benjamin Hoff
The Tao of Pooh

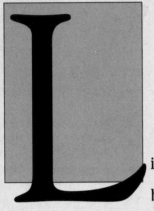ife for me is not black and white, but instead a million shades of gray, which continue to change. One of the first problems that right-brain-dominant people must address in the area of priorities is knowing how to determine what is most important. The divergent mind is great at generating quantity, but it has a difficult time remembering what has been generated. It needs a system for seeing all of the tasks that have been identi-

fied and their relative importance to one another. If there is no system in place for this "big picturing" to happen, right-brained people will just get started on the last item put on the list and forget about important ongoing projects that were created two weeks ago. It's not that they don't want to do them, but that the "out-of-sight, out-of-mind" syndrome takes over. This not only can be a problem for the right-brainers; it turns into a big problem for the people they work with, too. People with divergent minds can create ten times as many tasks as they and their colleagues combined can complete.

THE "I'LL THINK UP LOTS OF THINGS—YOU DO THEM" BATTLE

What we are describing is not just a hypothetical situation; it is a real dilemma my business partner, Duane Trammell, and I experienced that could have ended our partnership. My long suit is to come up with dozens of creative ideas that require someone to take action. Duane's strength is implementation; he makes notes on all our ideas and puts them into motion.

In the first year of our partnership, Duane came in one morn-

> *One never notices what has been done; one can only see what remains to be done.*
> —Madame Curie

ing with a thick stack of colored index cards. On each he had printed a major task I had suggested with a time estimate and resources needed. As he spread out the cards, he explained that he had two months of implementation work to do in two weeks. Finding himself working longer and getting further behind, he asked for my help in knowing which tasks were most important so he could focus on them and get his life back into balance. He felt frazzled and was beginning to resent my abundant imagination, which kept adding a new supply of tasks for him to follow up on.

This problem is not unique to Duane and myself; it plagues any team, department, or family in which there are two kinds of thinkers. For me (the divergent thinker), the fun was in coming up with new ideas. In fact, when I get tired or overwhelmed, I typically generate a new batch of possibilities. In my mind, they aren't automatically something we have to do but rather options that we might consider. For Duane (the convergent thinker), once we agree on a task or approach, his commitment is to get it done. Generating more possibilities only boxes him in tighter, especially when he can't see how we could possibly complete the first list of projects. The convergent thinker's joy and satisfaction comes from completing tasks. The divergent person's joy comes from generating new tasks.

These opposite traits, which have the potential for enormous creative synergy, have an equal potential for enormous destructive mismatching.

LOOK AT INDIVIDUAL TASKS IN CONTEXT WITH THE BIG PICTURE

The first strategy in solving this problem is to create a visual system that allows you to see all the tasks in relation to one another. As we spread out the index cards, Duane asked me to arrange them in order of importance, with A's the most important, B's next, and C's the least important. At first glance they all seemed to be A's. I started pushing to the top of the table the tasks that seemed most important and to the bottom those that were least urgent. Note that I could not put them in a linear sequence. I

HELP!

URGENT!

IMPORTANT!

CRITICAL

MOST IMPORTANT

NOW!

VERY URGENT

FAS

would still be struggling with the task if I had to complete it that way, for the A-B-C approach is a convergent, left-brained process. My strength is divergent, big-picture thinking, in which many pieces of information are juggled simultaneously.

The first ordering was easy, because it was obvious that some of the to-do's were brainstorming ideas that were not urgent or important; I dropped these ideas to the bottom. The more difficult task was looking at all of the A's that needed to be done first. But as we discussed the importance of each task together, we both learned new information that helped to establish its priority. For example, when I was reminded that income was low for September, we decided that the business-prospecting trip to Chicago should get priority over the seminar I wanted to attend in Seattle. We also could see that proposal writing took precedence over the performance reviews.

All of these tasks were of major importance, but seeing them together made the difference. By looking at all of the tasks at one time, we could focus on current company goals and consider each task's importance relative to these goals.

TOO MUCH TO DO AND NOT ENOUGH TIME

It would be great if the prioritizing challenges of business today could be solved with a stack of index cards, but they are much more complex. Nothing is permanent or stands still anymore. Every decision, to-do task, and major project is relative and is affected by every other change, shift in the schedule, cash-flow factor, or market demand. Tom Peters describes it as the world "going bonkers." He says, "In short, today's organizational images stink. Not just those that derive from the military ('Kick ass and take names') and 'pyramids' (heavy, steep, immobile), but even the new 'network,' 'spider web,' 'Calder mobile.' These modern notions are a mighty step forward, but they still miss the core idea of tomorrow's surviving corporation: dynamism. How about company-as-carnival?"

To support such a chaotic, carnival-like world, a new level of flexibility is required, we must have the ability to instantly reprioritize on a continuing basis, and we must develop improved habits of continually communicating and updating information with our teams.

E-mail, voice mail, and fax

machines open our updating capabilities to twenty-four hours of on-line, "living" information, but to survive, we need to learn to think in paradox. Knowing when we need to be "off-line" (off-duty, off the computer) is as important as staying constantly available.

In recent years, downsizing trends have become a way of life. Many people have found themselves responsible for a job description that two or even three people used to have. There will always be more to do than can be done by one person. How do people handle this situation? Here are some tips from people who are doing it successfully.

Trust Is the Key

Jim Wimberly, vice president of ground operations for Southwest Airlines Company, says this:

"People who are only doing the work of two people are loafing in our company. It doesn't matter whether it's two full-time jobs, four, or twelve that one person has to do. Our productivity is the result of the trust we have with each other. If you have the right trust, working relationship, and environment, the work gets done! I feel for companies trying to change from the old ways, but it can be done."

Consider Outsourcing

Another Southwest Airlines professional, Ann Rhoades, vice president of the People Department, tells how they use retired people to get more done:

"We have so many projects going on that we use a number of temporary employees. For example, we have three mailings per year that go out to 13,000 employees. For the past few years it would take twelve to twenty-four people seven to ten days to complete. This year we were approached by a group of retired people. They knocked us off our chairs with their incredible productivity. Five retirees, with average ages of

People with divergent minds can create ten times as many tasks as they and their colleagues combined can complete.

sixty to seventy years, completed the task in three days! And they insisted on coming in on New Year's Day and brought champagne to make it fun. They wanted to get the information out to the employees as early as possible.

"We were flabbergasted! How did they do it? Whereas the earlier groups wanted to make the task last as long as possible, these people came ready to be as productive as they possibly could be, challenging themselves to beat their own record."

Rethink Processes

Ric Hinkie, president of Midwest Gas Association, reports:

"When I came three years ago, we were a 'top down' model. The responsible manager and his 'girl Friday' did every step again and again. Instead of three teams of two, we became one team of six. One support person became responsible for all of the mailing lists, another took registrations, and another packed materials and got mailings out. The new system allowed managers to work with three different people to get their meetings promoted and organized. Each was still accountable, but they were a part of a less isolated process. The work force innovations

began. They weren't as linear. The whole change developed added pride in the employees and recognition by other staff and even our members (customers). Innovations continue as support people now have the time to plan meal functions, review speaker tapes, and perform other, more interesting tasks. The managers can now spend more time reviewing member issues like new governmental regulations, environmental updates, and re-engineering processes."

Seek Constant Feedback

According to Linda Conger, manager of the SCS Academy, The SABRE Group, a division of AMR Corporation, located in Dallas/Fort Worth:

"We are responsible for the customer service line. We brainstorm how we can eliminate some of the phone calls by getting curious about what we can change to prevent the problems that trigger the calls. It's important to think in four dimensions, not only to create a solution for the customer on the line, but after the fact to correct the problem that led to the call. We estimate that we are saving two to three hours per week with changes we have made based on questions

resolved through new service changes. The key is to stay close to our customers."

COMBINE TASKS TO SHORTEN THE LIST

A second strategy that helps to make the big priorities more manageable when there are still too many of them and not enough time consists of combining tasks, or *compounding*. This is such an important strategy that we have devoted an entire chapter to it later in the book (see Chapter Fourteen). But for now, I want to give you a quick version of this strategy that will help you in prioritizing.

As you survey all of the tasks that need to be done, ask yourself the following two questions:

1. Could I work on any of these tasks while I am doing something else?

2. Do any of these tasks overlap so that I could combine them into one project and still accomplish both sets of goals?

I have found this skill to be invaluable. Many times, I draft proposals on an airplane flight. Phone calls can be returned in the car. Other tasks can be combined in more imaginative ways:

- Instead of conducting a separate market test for a book design, I show examples of designs to seminar or conference attendees during breaks, over lunch, and at the end of the day to get a variety of opinions.

- Two writing projects can be combined into one: copy requested by a client for an upcoming seminar flyer can be edited to serve as one of the sections in a new proposal for another client.

- A magazine writer requesting a three-hour interview can be invited to a scheduled seminar, with twenty minutes allowed for questions at the end.

Ellen Kent, corporate planning manager of Herman Miller, Inc., in Grand Rapids, Michigan, combines tasks from her to-do list with her commute to and from work:

"I do voice-mail messaging while I drive my commute. Also, having a notepad on my dashboard provides visual reminders of what to do the next day or whom to call."

With some creative thinking, an unmanageable list of priorities can usually be made more manageable.

DO IT "QUICK AND DIRTY"

A third prioritizing strategy is to decide in advance how much time and effort you can afford to give each task. We would all like to perform each task at the level of greatest excellence possible, but time limitations prohibit us from doing this. We use the phrase "quick and dirty" to describe tasks that require speed more than perfection. These words give you permission to lower your standards in order to do the job faster. They can keep you from falling into the trap of using outdated work methods when you feel behind and overwhelmed.

Here are two examples of creative shifts into the "quick and dirty" mode. Notice that the result can be even more creative and appropriate than if the task had been done the "perfect" way.

1. One of our team members typically prepares a large folding collage of photographs of clients with background colors and relevant quotes. These create a great instant review of our previous sessions and a stimulating, appealing learning environment. One day when we were pushed for time, she found an attractive basket and

> ## *H*ard work is often the easy work you did not do at the proper time.
>
> —Bernard Meltzer
> *Bernard Meltzer's Guidance for Living*

napkin and put all the photos in the basket. Above the basket she put the collage board and a glue stick with a sign inviting, "Post Your Favorite." This took ten minutes in place of the usual hour and a half and the clients enjoyed the change of pace.

2. Another big time-saver is drafting our proposals "quick and dirty." One of us begins a fast draft. Usually this is a mind map of ideas for our team to build on. Next, a partner polishes it, and a third team member edits and critiques it. We may then be ready to format a clean draft and fax it to the client for feedback. We've found that by keeping the proposal in draft form for so long,

all of us are more willing to suggest totally new approaches than we would have been if the first person had presented a polished, time-consuming, completed proposal.

Another interesting paradox is that "quick and dirty" often leads to a significant improvement in performance, using interdependent teaming at its best.

ALLOW SOME TASKS TO DIE A NATURAL DEATH

A final prioritizing strategy is what I call "natural prioritizing." If an item remains on my list of less important items for a couple of months, I declare it dead and have a brief moment of silence to honor its passing. Then I throw it out with whatever appendages are tied to it, such as guilt and remorse. This is the idea of Dave Wilson, national director of professional development at Ernst & Young (a brilliant friend who is wonderfully funny, creative, productive, and highly respected in his field).

It took us a while to come to these conclusions about how right- and left-brain-dominant people see and understand priorities, and in the process, we made a game out of the whole matter. The important thing is to recognize when your highly prolific imagination is acting as a trap for yourself and others, and then to use the four strategies to climb out of that trap.

WHEN *YOUR* PRIORITIES BECOME *MY* PRIORITIES

Many companies are using new calendar software programs on networks so that schedules are on the computer with open access by others. Although this can be helpful to others in planning, it can play havoc with our personal priorities. If there is an open slot, suddenly your priority to have me at a meeting can override my priority to prepare for a presentation. Some executives we work with have come up with a way to protect unscheduled time. They may add extra time on either side of appointments or they may even "schedule" an appointment with a colleague who then happens to cancel at the last minute. Blocking out extra time helps them keep the work, planning, and thinking time they need between meetings as a priority.

A related idea came from a busy executive with long hours

and a heavy travel schedule who found that home and family time kept getting pushed aside. After a late evening of client entertaining, he now schedules a "breakfast meeting" without specifying who it's with. Then he invites his wife to breakfast on the deck, in bed, or at a special restaurant so they keep their own quality time woven into their busy life.

"She's always willing to pitch in at a moment's notice to help with client entertaining," he says. "Why shouldn't I make sure she feels recognized and special and invest the same quality and excellence in our partnership that I would with a client?"

You can't create quality on the job if you aren't creating it equally in your personal life. If

you keep good things happening there, you'll return to work with more creative energy, commitment, and imagination.

A final tip is to review your schedule and ask what is *not* on your list that is a priority for your personal balance and excellence. Often we only write down commitments to others, forgetting commitments to ourselves. The magic of deep, sustaining balance comes from living on the basis of our core values rather than getting hooked into simply doing what's on our list.

You can't create quality on the job if you don't create it equally in your personal life.

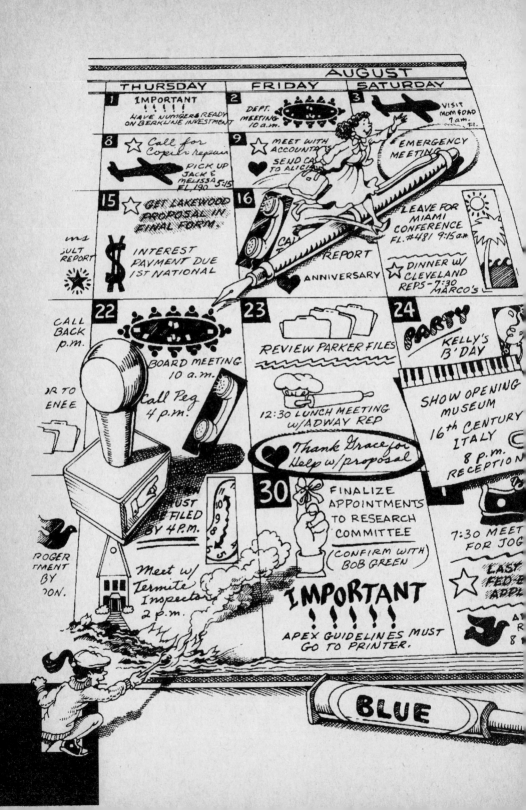

SCHEDULING: Making Your CALENDAR FUN AND FUNCTIONAL

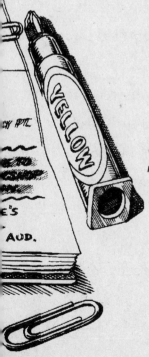

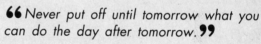
66 Never put off until tomorrow what you can do the day after tomorrow. **99**

—Mark Twain

66 I've been on a calendar, but never on time. **99**

—Marilyn Monroe

66 Nothing is particularly hard if you divide it into small jobs. **99**

—Henry Ford

o you've got your to-do list under control and have identified some
priorities that need your attention for
the day or week. Next, you need to
decide when you can work on these
tasks and still remember the other important meetings, phone calls, and appointments you have committed to, as well as
making room for the unexpected emergencies
that crowd into any busy day. Now you are ready
to design your scheduling system.

IT'S CHRISTMAS—
BUY YOURSELF A PRESENT!

The first step will be fun: go to an office supply store and pick out a calendar that fits your style. Remember that there are dozens of formats to choose from that schedule a day, a week, or a month at a time. They come in a small pocket size, a small desk size, a notebook desk size, and a poster size for wall calendars.

In making your decision, think about which type of calendar you are more likely to keep up with and write in:

- If you are on the go or travel frequently, as much as you may like the large desk size, it will probably be too cumbersome to travel with. You'll probably want a pocket size, or something that will easily fit into your travel briefcase.

- If you need to make note of other people's schedules that affect yours, you might want a larger format with more space to write.

- If you usually work from your desk and enjoy computers, you might consider some of the new software programs that are scheduling tools. You can print out a hard copy of your schedule or take it to your meetings as needed. But be advised! It takes quite a bit of self-discipline to key in changes and additions to these calendar programs. It might sound like fun at first, but be honest with yourself about the likelihood of your sticking with all of the detail work required to keep an up-to-date calendar on disk.

Another option for calendar purchase is to call Day-Timers at 215-266-9000 and request a catalog for a banquet of options, both practical and fun. Regardless of where you purchase your new calendar, the point is to find one that you really like, buy it, and enjoy using it.

MAKE YOUR CALENDAR
VISUAL AND FUN

One of the key strategies for making a calendar work for those of us who are right-brain-dominant is to allow it to be highly visual and fun. The right brain processes and "sees" information differently from the left brain. In order for information to register with the right brain, it must stand apart—it has to look different from the rest of the page.

You can make abstract information look different on your calendar pages by:

- Adding color
- Changing the size or style of your writing
- Drawing pictures or symbols
- Flagging important information with dot codes
- Adding stickers or picture symbols to your calendar slots
- Using Post-it Notes to represent time-flexible activities or events

USE COLOR TO BLOCK OUT EVENTS

Use brightly colored highlighters to draw colored boxes around the categories of events, tasks, or activities you have written in your calendar. Develop your own personal color-coding system. We use the following system for our calendars:

Travel time for your trips out of town (too much yellow back-to-back signals potential problems)

Events or presentations that require lots of planning and rehearsal time (special preplanning is needed if pink is back-to-back)

Meetings or appointments that require lit-tle or no preparation

Personal work time

Time for fun, play, and relaxation

USE POST-IT NOTES TO BUILD IN FLEXIBILITY

We use Post-it Notes in two ways. When events are tentative, we write them on a Post-it Note and put them on the calendar or appointment square. When a client or friend requests a schedule change, no problem! We just move the note and no additional paperwork is required.

ADD COLORED DOTS AND FUN STICKERS

Colored self-adhesive dots (found in any office supply store) can be used on your calendar to call attention to important events. Develop a code that makes sense to you. For example, we use red dots to signal a deadline or promise date and green for financial updates.

Use neat little stickers to celebrate and reward yourself while you work to make a new behavior an automatic habit. We found tiny, brightly colored hearts to use on days when we eat healthy food or enjoy aerobics. (It's important to make exercise fun for the right brain and not just suffer through it. The brain chemicals generated from fun are just as important as the shift in metabolism that comes from exercise.)

We also enjoy using shiny little stars when we tackle or complete a big task. Try drawing little cartoons across vacation days or holidays; I have little cartoons that signal cross-country skiing and the Balloon Festival in Albuquerque, New Mexico.

Of course, if you get compulsive about stickers, you can squelch or spoil the fun they can bring to your system! Use them to keep your right brain interested

Another way to use Post-it Notes on the calendar is to list tasks that can be done anytime during the week. As scheduled events change or your mood alters, you can move the task to a time that works better for you.

> **It's the good girls who keep the diaries; the bad girls never have the time.**
>
> —Tallulah Bankhead

in planning and scheduling and to personalize your system. Don't turn them into another job.

One last word on calendars: You may find that you need to switch calendars if you lose interest in the one you are using. Several years ago I noticed a client using a nifty calendar, but it was August and I still had four months on the one I was using. Then it occurred to me that the improved efficiency in my system would be worth more than the dollars saved by sticking with my current calendar. A divergent personality craves change just for the fun of trying something different. So now I allow myself to change systems whenever I get bored and notice myself procrastinating on follow-through. Just by appreciating and responding to this

unique need, I find myself more consistent and cooperative toward the organizational requirements in my life.

LEARN TO SEE INVISIBLE TIME

Once the options have been narrowed to a single calendar, there are still some potholes along the way for right-brained, divergent thinkers. Being big-picture thinkers, we are apt to schedule the event on the calendar, but be unrealistic about how much time is actually involved. In our enthusiasm for the idea, we forget about the time it takes to prepare for the event and make it happen. Here are some tasks or activities requiring extra time that are important to block out on your calendar, but are typically forgotten:

- *Driving time to an in-town appointment.* Plan for an extra twenty minutes in addition to the regular driving time to allow for traffic jams and parking problems.

- *Flying time to an out-of-town appointment.* Allow an extra two hours before the appointment for flight delays and, when possible, arrange to fly in the night before.

- *Incoming phone calls.* Depending on how much time you need to be available to others, this could be one to two hours or more. Leave pockets of time between scheduled appointments, even on busy days.

- *Reading mail, going through your in-basket, and responding to queries.* Schedule varying amounts of time for this task, perhaps from thirty to forty-five minutes.

- *Personal planning time.* Schedule fifteen to thirty minutes of planning time at the beginning of the day to organize yourself and reconsider important priorities for the day.

- *People development, questions, problem solving, and mentoring.* Leave pockets of time for interacting with others.

- *Preparation for commitments.* Some of these tasks might include preparing an agenda before leading a meeting, packing or unpacking from a trip, planning with partners before meeting a client, or planning with your family before a party at home. Life will go more smoothly when you allow time to communicate and to accomplish these invisible but necessary preparations.

Two easy ways to make yourself aware of these often-overlooked key steps are:

1. Harvest and learn from your past, overcrowded days. What kinds of tasks didn't you plan for that you might schedule into your day?

2. Ask a convergent partner, whose long suit is planning, to coach you on the kinds of maintenance activities you typically overlook or fail to schedule time for.

SCHEDULE FOR ENERGY AS WELL AS TIME

As you work with your calendar, it is important to take note of the type of activity you are scheduling and the kind of

Get as good at preplanning fun as you are now at scheduling work.

energy it will require. We often look at a calendar and see only blank spaces to be filled, without considering our personal needs. Each of us has times during the day when our physical and mental energy peaks and ebbs. Make it a point to schedule the most demanding, taxing, and challenging tasks during the time of day when you have the most energy. Save tasks such as filing, reviewing mail, writing a personal thank-you note, or returning telephone calls for low-energy times when you need to coast a bit. And to maintain health, effectiveness, and enthusiasm for the long haul, pay attention to your body's signals, like hunger, fatigue, and the need for a change of pace.

In our business we find that even if there is open time on the calendar, we do ourselves and our clients a disservice when we schedule our seminars back-to-back without leaving ourselves time for planning and recovery between sessions.

Seminars and client presentations demand a great deal of physical, mental, and emotional energy from those making the presentations. In our office, the working day is normally extended from 6:00 A.M. to 11:00 P.M. on seminar days. Much of the time is spent standing or performing physical tasks, including moving, unload-ing, and loading heavy boxes, climbing several flights of stairs, setting up stage effects using walls and high ceilings, quickly changing a room set up for 250 to accommodate 400, and standing in front of hot lights all day.

These days usually offer difficult situations to be solved, some with emotional overtones. In addition, there is the overarching stress of trying to present a successful program while constantly being under scrutiny, and of making everything work. It is important to balance this type of energy requirement with a day back in

Schedule the most demanding, taxing, and challenging tasks during the time of day when you have the most energy.

122

the office or, if you are traveling, with different kinds of meetings or projects following a seminar. Every business or career has similar situations.

So as you put items on your calendar, think not just about how much time an actual task may take, but also about the kind and amount of energy it will require. Develop some way to signal these demands on your calendar. (Color-coding our calendar allows us to assess our balance at a glance.) Then, as you make your schedule, you'll have a visual reminder not to stack high-demand activities one after the other to the point where you are exhausted and not doing anything well.

TIME COMES IN ALL SHAPES AND SIZES

One challenge we all face is that our real work time doesn't come packaged in the nice, neat, uninterrupted blocks that are on the calendar. People who make progress have learned how to use fragmented time as well as larger segments of uninterrupted time; they also are good at discovering overlooked pockets of time. Here are some examples.

Fragments of Time

You are waiting for phone calls to be returned and you may have five minutes or forty minutes.

This is a good time to review mail, update your calendar, make short notes or reminders to yourself for later, draft brief pieces of correspondence, or leave quick messages on voice mail.

Refresh yourself with a joy break, stretch, daydream, meditate, flip through a Far Side cartoon book. Don't think of this as wasting time. Renewal is essential if you expect to achieve long-term, high-quality performance.

Some time-management systems call these "C tasks," low-priority tasks you should omit in order to save time for the high-priority items. There can be wisdom in this, but I find that by using these broken pieces of time for smaller tasks, I can build my energy, network, and gain long-term benefits.

Clear, Uninterrupted Time

The phone is not as busy, or you can have someone hold your calls.

Save this precious time for high-priority tasks such as work-

123

ing on major projects or taking the opportunity for deep thinking, resolving conflicts, or coaching team members.

Linda Haneborg, vice president for corporate communications for Express Services in Oklahoma City, tells how her company creates this kind of time:

"Four days a week, from 3:00 to 4:00 P.M., we have our 'Quiet Time.' All the office doors are closed, and each person respects the time of others. We cannot always observe Quiet Time, but when it's implemented, it provides time to organize, reorganize, think, read, regroup, and create. Of course, important phone calls are still routed through and important meetings are still held."

Overlooked Pockets of Time

This is time that is not obviously free, but that can be put to use if you've planned for it.

For waiting time, keep a folder of articles or clippings that you never have time to read in the office, and pull them out when you are stuck. Travel time can be some of the best uninterrupted work time; we have learned to treasure it.

Becky Rush, vice president of regional operations for The Prudential in Houston, agrees:

"I'm sitting here typing this on the plane. I have found my laptop computer to be a great time-saver. Before, I could convince myself to do some reading but little else. Now I can complete work and enjoy getting it done. On the flight back from New Jersey to Houston this time, I've done three performance reviews, which I would have had to try to do at other times in a very hectic schedule."

COORDINATE SCHEDULES IN A TEAM

Team scheduling is a topic that needs an entire book to do justice to it. No matter how carefully we lay out our personal plans, almost everyone is affected by other people's schedules. Following are some tips that we have learned from our clients.

Betsy Harrison, president of Career Development Services in Rochester, New York, explains what works for her organization:

"We have an organization of fifty people; of those, forty-six are women! We are not caught up in hierarchy. The spiderweb model is

the norm. We are an interconnected team. We all work many hours each week with evening responsibilities as well. The key is in taking care of each other and encouraging the necessary rest and family and personal time. Many of us use a scheduling approach that I call 'The Whole Life Calendar.' Everything is included on our calendars, not just work. If it is a personal priority to get to a child's soccer game or to spend quality time with aging parents, it gets put on the calendar so all aspects of our lives can be supported by the team. Most important, we have put the systems in place to support this commitment, such as flextime and flex benefit programs.

"We also have a task force to deal with issues of internal communication, and many great recommendations have resulted, such as decisions about what's appropriate for voice mail (births, major illnesses, new contracts) and what's not appropriate (vacations, a favorite fund-raiser, minor illnesses). These items are put in our in-house newsletter, 'The Grapevine.' Other recommendations have included instituting 'Lunch and Learn' luncheons and the goal that we each go to lunch annually with at least two people on staff with whom we do not have regular contact.

"Most often, when we have a problem, we can trace it back to a lack of communication. So we underscore taking personal responsibility for informing each other and for staying in touch. In that way, we never have to say, 'Nobody told me.' "

The most universal complaint from every company we work with is meetings and their tendency to be a time waster. Many executives must travel frequently to quarterly or monthly meetings. Donna Knox, executive vice president of Focus Networks Satellite Communication in Dallas, tells us that many companies are using technology to make these meetings more time-efficient. She reports:

"By linking up locations electronically, Saks, Macy's, and other companies are saving time, keeping key people accessible, and involving more people in the decision and information process. The designers can speak directly to front-line sales associates and can even field questions, learn consumer responses and needs, and instantly correct problems."

Jim Kouzes, president of Tom Peters Group/Learning Systems in Palo Alto, California, tells about a creative way his group handles informational meetings:

"Of all the company-wide activities, the one that most facilitates staying up-to-date with ongoing projects is something that we refer to as 'The Huddle.' The Huddle is a weekly meeting that is called early in the week, usually on a Monday or Tuesday morning, by the receptionist. She announces it over the intercom, and everyone assembles around the front desk. We huddle there so the receptionist can participate and still answer phones when they ring.

"We each take turns, and in about two minutes we provide the most current information on whatever is pressing. Someone might report on a recent sale, the next theme for our subscription newsletter, praise from a customer, a customer problem, the need for help on a project, the new health care plan, or whatever is urgent.*

"We used to produce written weekly reports, but most folks complained about having to do them. Not so with The Huddle. Even though much of our business comes from our writing, when it comes to staying up-to-date, we clearly prefer the verbal and interactive."

No matter how carefully we lay out our personal plans, almost everyone is affected by other people's schedules.

One last thought. If you are lucky enough to have assistants, secretaries, or work partners of any type, involve them in your time management system. Many misunderstandings and problems concerning time occur between partners because they are working out of different assumptions. Meet together and make decisions on these points:

- When and how often will you meet to coordinate and update schedules?

- How can you make entries on your calendar?

- How can your assistant help protect your schedule?

- Who sets the priorities?

126

■ What can you do to help your assistant or work partners be more effective?

Carl Conger, manager of applications systems maintenance, Information Technology, for Texas Utilities in Dallas, shares his belief in communicating very directly and telling people in advance what works and doesn't work:

"I give my direct reports permission to insist on timeliness and responsiveness from me. If they need me, I expect them to grab me, get on my calendar, even write themselves in on my calendar. Don't say to me, 'I need to see you sometime' or 'I need this as soon as you can get to it.' That vagueness is dangerous to a polychronic person. If you need something by 5:00 P.M. Thursday, make sure that gets said."

Lucy Billingsley, of Billingsley Company, a partner in the Wyndham Travel Management Company in Dallas, tells us how she works with her assistants:

"I don't put limits on myself, and I don't expect that there is anything others who work with me can't do. I work with three assis-tants and I delegate generously, so I need people who will make me aware when they are in overload so we can create options to accomplish our goals and preserve our resources—them.

"In communication I, the sender, am responsible for the 'catch' of the accurate message. If they miss, it probably has to do with how I 'pitched' it. I used to blame the receiver. Now I have learned to look at my role in it; perhaps I gave, or didn't give, materials and information in such a way that it crippled their ability to perform.

"One last area I am focusing on (but where I still have many opportunities to improve) is tak-ing the time to give assistants the context in assignments. It is the most effective way to improve their ability to perform at higher levels, but the easiest to overlook. I look for ways to include them in key meetings. This builds their infor-mation base, confidence, credibil-ity, and motivation. Less time needs to be spent later because they were in on the initial transaction. So instead of telling them what to do, I can get their ideas and we can agree on the next move. This makes their work so much more interest-ing that they will create ways to cover their other responsibilities in order to be there when they are needed."

SCHEDULE YOUR PLAY AS CAREFULLY AS YOU DO YOUR WORK!

Do you remember when you were courting how clever you were at making everything fun and designing little treats and surprises? Do you remember the magic of your energy, motivation, and productivity when you were madly in love? That was no accident. It was a great example of the unrealized potential we have for energizing work with play.

Get as good at preplanning fun as you are now at scheduling work. Teri Hires, senior vice president and managing director of the Dallas office, Drake Beam Morin, Inc., tells this story:

"February was going to be a very demanding month, so we decided to do something playful as a team with our spouses. After some discussion, we signed up for push dance lessons at Brookhaven Community College. We persuaded them to create a class just for our team. Who would have believed that having fun together on Sunday evenings would transform our energy and teaming. We have become more productive, flexible, and mutually supportive as a result of our shared fun."

Make it a point to add play-time all through your calendar, and then notice the significant improvement in energy, enthusiasm, flexibility, teamwork, and productivity you experience. Creative, balancing play can be worth a lot!

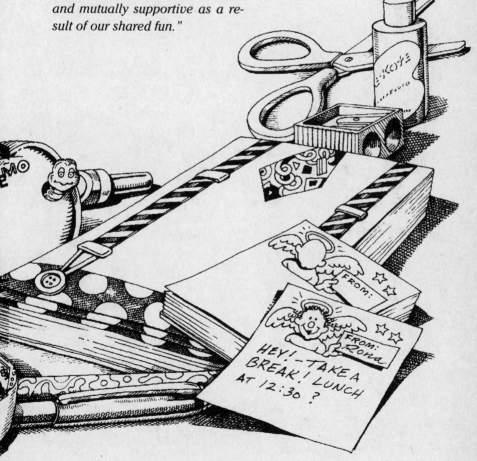

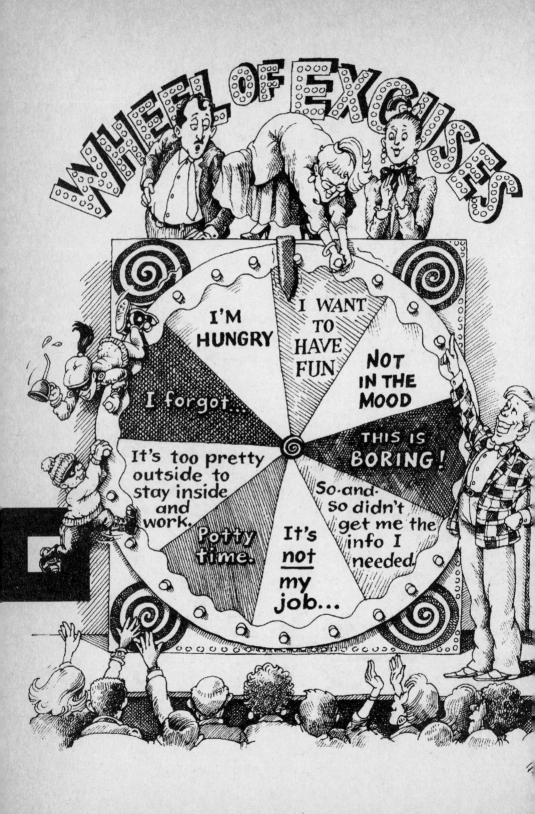

11

FOLLOWING YOUR PLAN:
How to STICK TO IT
When You'd *Rather* Move on
to New Ideas

> **66** *Eighty percent of life is just showing up.* **99**
> —Woody Allen

> **66** *If at first you don't succeed, try, try again. Then quit. There's no use being a damn fool about it.* **99**
> —W. C. Fields

> **66** *I have so much to do that I am going to bed.* **99**
> —Savoyard proverb

131

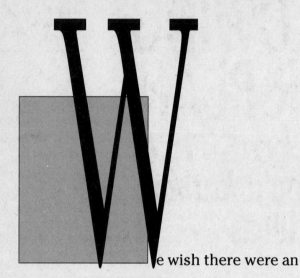

e wish there were an
easy answer to the problems right-brained,
divergent people face when they get to this
last step of traditional time management,
but unfortunately, there aren't any easy
answers. However, we will share some
of our insights, and you can decide
which ones can help you in this
troublesome area of follow-through.
We will first explore typical traps
for the divergent thinker and will
then suggest several ways to
escape them.

"I FORGOT WHAT I WAS SUPPOSED TO BE WORKING ON"

This seems a little absurd, yet it is one of the primary reasons why right-brained people don't follow through on their work. The divergent mind is so involved in generating new thoughts that what was written on a planning list or daily calendar on Monday is forgotten history on Wednesday. Sometimes it is forgotten history at mid-morning on Monday!

The first step is to make sure your to-do list and schedule are in plain sight. Use any of the visual techniques that we described in the last three chapters to keep this important information in front of you. Make it a habit to consciously look at the list and schedule each morning or the evening before. Link it to a morning task you look forward to—for example, you might review it while enjoying a cup of coffee or herb tea.

Another strategy is to purposely set up a fifteen-minute meeting the first thing in the morning with your secretary, a colleague, or another person on your team. Review your plans jointly so that you get a good solid picture in your memory of what you need to be doing for the next eight hours.

"IT'S THOSE INTERRUPTIONS THAT GET ME OFF TASK"

You've reviewed your list, know what priority project you are working on, and are sitting at your desk ready to begin it. Then the telephone rings . . . or the unexpected visitor comes in the office . . . or your assistant needs help on a letter that must go out . . . or a colleague wants to talk about a political situation she is caught up in between her boss and another department. Your best intentions to work on the project go out the window. What do you do about things you have no control over?

The first question to ask yourself is: "Do I *really* have no control over these interruptions?" Be honest. Some are most likely unavoidable, but think about the others. Your right brain may just be taking over. Remember that the right brain loves new stimuli, new tasks, new interactions with people, and yes, even new crises. All of these things are a lot more challenging and fun than sitting at a desk working on the same old project you started fifteen minutes ago. If you aren't careful, the right brain will use any interruption as an excuse to get away from the project or task at hand. You have several options here depending on how frolicsome your little-kid right brain is.

If you know that you are a talker and can get caught on the phone for thirty minutes or more, consider having your calls held, except for the urgent ones, and devote an hour before lunch returning them. Weigh your priorities. Is it more fun helping others than getting your own work done? Which is most important? The choice will be different for each interruption. You might request a conference later in the day once you have the gist

of what the other person needs. I find that blocking out time to get certain projects done helps me, and keeping this visual, colorful plan in front of me constantly reminds me of my commitments and options.

The phone dilemma deserves some discussion here. The phone is the great disrupter of schedules. Here are some tips we have collected from friends and clients:

- Schedule lengthy phone calls just as if they were meetings: call ahead or ask your assistant to call ahead to set a time for the call.

- Convert your random incoming calls to "phone dates." Instead of rushing to get off the line because you don't have time to talk, arrange for a better time to talk and you will make the caller feel valued instead of discounted.

- Keep commitments and eliminate phone tag by scheduling follow-up calls at the end of your conversation. Instead of saying "I'll get back to you about this next week," say "I'll work on having an answer for you on Tuesday, and even if I don't, I'll check in with you. Can we schedule a call for three o'clock?"

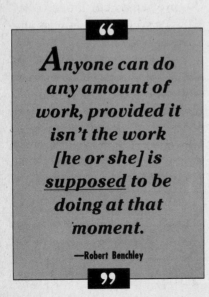

Anyone can do any amount of work, provided it isn't the work [he or she] is supposed to be doing at that moment.

—Robert Benchley

Our last piece of advice comes from Vivian Cosey, general manager of human resources, Ryerson Coil Processing of Chicago:

"I am amazed at the number of people who think that whenever a phone rings, it must be answered at that exact moment. Many calls that come through in the course of the day are low-priority requests or from people who just want to chat. But since most people can't stand the sound of that ringing phone, they have a knee-jerk response to answer it, even if they are in the middle of something important. I have trained myself to be able to not hear it. I also have found that I can increase my productivity by screening calls through an answering system at certain periods when I will benefit from uninterrupted blocks of time."

"I NEED SOMETHING FROM SOMEONE ELSE BEFORE I CAN PROCEED"

Right-brained thinkers may also be sidetracked from an important task if we need some information from a colleague or another department and believe we can't go any further until we get it. The right brain loves this. It

isn't our fault, and now we get to stop and do something new.

One way to keep the momentum is to go ahead and block in what you can do, using what you know. Leave blanks for the missing information. It can be added later, perhaps by somebody else. A gentle nudge to the person you are waiting for might also help, so that you can be sure the information is coming and has not been forgotten. Or ask yourself, "What else can I do to keep the priorities moving?"

"I'M JUST NOT IN THE MOOD"

You've checked your list, know what you need to produce, have the time, and are free from interruptions—but you're fresh out of creative ideas for the new employee orientation meeting (or whatever is to be done). Your right brain confirms the dilemma and whispers in your ear, "This is hopeless. You can sit here all morning and never get anywhere. Let's do something else and we'll come back to it later."

This switch-to-another-task strategy is okay if you have plenty of time, but what if a draft is due by 2:00 P.M. today? Before your right brain gets away, start a dialogue with it and ask, "What would it take to get you in a great mood?" Here are some strategies that we use:

- Call someone who is good at what you are working on and get his or her ideas on the project.

- *Use mental bookends.* Image by bracketing a chosen event with specific, positive expectations before and after it happens, like bookends bracing a row of books. Take three slow, deep breaths and relax into a wonderful fantasy in which you have just the right inspiration, come up with dynamite ideas, enjoy the process because you know you are producing wonderful work, and complete a highly successful project. Then open your eyes and, keeping the same positive mood, launch into your project.

- *Fast-forward.* Weigh your options, or fast-forward your imagination to visualize why you will benefit from the task at hand. Ask yourself what part it plays in your overall goals and dreams? What's the worst thing that can happen if you don't do it? By fitting this immediate decision into the big

picture, you can often change your perspective. Knowing the options and alternatives, you are ready to work.

- *Just get started!* When I'm not in the mood to be creative and think I'm totally dry, I'm often amazed what comes out if I just start any old way.

"BORING, BORING, BORING . . . THIS ISN'T FUN ANYMORE"

Think of income tax returns. Unless you are a certified public accountant who sees a blank Form 1040 as a bare canvas begging for a creative flurry of numbers, chances are you are going to get very tired of separating receipts before the tax return is finished. The challenge is: How can you make a boring task that must be done more enjoyable? Better yet, how can you keep your right brain entertained so that it won't physically carry you away and abandon the whole project?

This is where combining positives with negatives can help you. Make a list of things that appeal to your right brain:

- Freshly baked chocolate-chip cookies

- Broadway show tunes

- *Casablanca*

- Brightly colored envelopes for sorting receipts

- Breaking up work periods with playful activities

- Translucent envelopes

- Jumbo colored clips

Then combine something from this list with part of your boring task. For example, you might listen to the musical score from *Les Misérables* while you are cleaning the bathroom or work on your mileage record while watching *The Big Chill*.

Another creative way you can weave positive momentum into what could be a negative energy drain is to trade out with a friend: if you help me with my taxes I'll fix a gourmet feast for you (or plant petunias in your garden, or whatever).

As your little-kid self learns that your task-driving self can be trusted to balance work with fun, you will get much better cooperation. When you are highly resistant and rebellious, you probably have mistreated your playful self and are joy-starved. You don't have to go home from work exhausted.

DEALING WITH THE THREE-YEAR-OLD INSIDE YOU

One important element in sticking with the plan is to stay refreshed with daily fun and renewal. When you are joy-starved, you become unmanageable and cantankerous. You feel like a reasonable, well-meaning adult, trapped inside an out-of-control three-year-old! But when you stay balanced with ample fun, exercise, and relaxation, you look forward to your daily planning meetings because you have enjoyed so much success as a result of the support they generate.

UNEXPECTED DETOURS

Detours from the plan can come in two forms: the detours that we choose ourselves and the detours that are caused by other people.

Procrastination is an interesting form of self-detour. Although it can have negative effects, not all procrastination is bad. In traditional time management, it has been assumed that getting rid of procrastination is always desirable, because procrastination will keep you from accomplishing your goals. Often

Reward Yourself!

Create ways to encourage and reward yourself for following through on plans, projects, and commitments. I make a plan each weekday morning, ensuring that there are always several joy breaks built into it. Then at the end of the day, I celebrate my gains.

By being curious about the times when I don't stick to my plan and exploring the reasons, I am improving my ability to stay on track.

138

this is true. If you hate to fill out expense reports and wait to complete them for seven trips until the last night before they are due, it would serve you well to create a new system that would help you to eliminate the procrastination. (Our solution to this is to fill the report out on the last leg of the flight back home; we find it makes the trip go faster.)

But we question the assumption that we need to get rid of all our procrastinating. We need some level of procrastination to balance the "ready, shoot, aim" mentality that surrounds us. Let's get curious about how procrastination might benefit us.

Incubation

Often, our intuition needs more time to incubate on a certain issue before we act. Many people learn that if they sleep on major decisions or difficult issues, they will typically come out with better solutions. I find that what I used to label procrastination in my own behavior was often the polychronic incubation time necessary to allow my creative juices to bubble sufficiently. But how long is long

enough? You never know until the idea finds you.

Waiting for Energy

Sometimes, when you have a big job to do, you may not have the kind of energy you need to tackle it and get it done. I often find that when I put things off until the last minute, the energy surge I get from the charge of adrenaline caused by being up against an almost impossible deadline gives me the boost to not just get the job done, but do it with excellence. Some people find that they can force risk by pushing deadlines and that their best work often occurs under self-imposed pressure.

One word of caution. If you constantly push your deadlines, you can burn out both yourself and others on your team. It's easy to become addicted to your own adrenaline and become unable to work effectively unless you are in the midst of a crisis. This is not a healthy life-style, and it can lead to long-term health problems. So proceed with caution.

Better Brain Waves

A shift in brain waves takes place when you are working in the wee hours of the morning. Have you ever found that the work or writing you do between 2:00 and 5:00 A.M. is much better than you can ever imagine yourself doing during regular working hours? I recall, when I was in school, making some of my best grades on papers that were written at the last moment during all-nighters.

Although it is a no-no to most people, deep fatigue can block the logic of traditional thinking and solutions. Some people find that they are far more likely to generate totally fresh, creative work during their second wind. The author of *Alice's Adventures in Wonderland,* Lewis Carroll, and other famous authors are known to have worked through many sleepless nights to generate the fantasies and intriguing stories that have lived on as timeless treasures. We must balance the potential benefits of late-night work with the downside—bleary eyes and gallons of caffeine.

Intuition Speaking

Some procrastination is our intuition telling us that this task may not be worth doing. Rather than jumping in and doing it right now, give it a couple of days to see if it is still a top priority. We have noticed that with client information changing so quickly, we actually can save time by holding off on some requests.

Although detours caused by outside forces, such as added clients or unexpected requests for new program designs, are challenging because they are not anticipated, they can also lead to better customer relations, improved services, and innovations. Sharon Melville, vice president of corporate services for Career Development Services, Rochester, New York, tells us:

"On our work plan (which we are rigorous about keeping updated) there is a page called 'Unexpected Detours' following each section. In today's world, one must allow for these. We reward flexibility by documenting what happened and what we did. This also helps us recognize those people who have flexible attitudes and are willing to pitch in to make a project work. We need people who thrive on change, can handle the unexpected, and work well in teams. We place a high value on this in our organization."

ENLIST THE HELP OF OTHERS

When you are a solo act, you limit what you can do.

But when you make personal shifts so that you can participate in whole-brained planning, you attract the support of other people who are strong where you are not. You can accomplish more because of the synergy of the group and can focus on expanding your gifts instead of staying stuck in your blind spots and weaknesses.

If you find that you typically ignore your plans and frustrate your family and co-workers because you plan with them, only to go in an opposite direction, forgive yourself! You are classically divergent in this trait. Knowing the reasons for your behavior helps. You do not have a fatal flaw in your character. You are not a terrible person because you don't like to follow through on your projects. In-

stead, you are a source of creativity, fresh ideas, and energy. When you know the causes of your actions, you can see ways to achieve greater satisfaction from the tasks you complete and find ways to work more harmoniously with others.

Invite those around you to remind you gently when you frustrate them by not honoring mutual plans. The "gently" part is critical. If others pound on you for your "failures," it is likely to trigger rebellion and resentment. You might suggest to them that it is easier for you to cooperate and return to a convergent plan if they can encourage and invite, rather than accuse and blame. Ask for what you want in advance and let others know when their positive encouragement helps you.

PART
Three

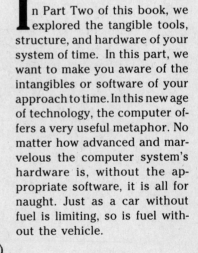

MENTAL SOFTWARE THAT UNCOVERS HIDDEN TIME

In Part Two of this book, we explored the tangible tools, structure, and hardware of your system of time. In this part, we want to make you aware of the intangibles or software of your approach to time. In this new age of technology, the computer offers a very useful metaphor. No matter how advanced and marvelous the computer system's hardware is, without the appropriate software, it is all for naught. Just as a car without fuel is limiting, so is fuel without the vehicle.

So shift your thinking as you have fun exploring and discovering some totally new ways of expanding your sense of time and its unlimited benefits for your life, joy, and productivity. For those of us in the quality movement, these are all tools for leveraging new excellence into our personal, family, and professional lives.

PERMISSION TO *Play*

12

> **❝** . . . reality is the leading cause of stress amongst those in touch with it. I can take it in small doses, but as a lifestyle I found it too confining. **❞**
>
> —Jane Wagner
> *The Search for Signs of Intelligent Life in the Universe*
> (as performed by Lily Tomlin in her one-woman show)

> **❝** Each person has [his or her] own safe place—running, painting, swimming, fishing, weaving, gardening. The activity itself is less important than the act of drawing on your own resources. **❞**
>
> —Barbara Gordon

> **❝** Each day, and the living of it, has to be a conscious creation in which discipline and order are relieved with some play and pure foolishness. **❞**
>
> —May Sarton

If you haven't gotten all your work finished you can't go out to play!" We may have heard this from a parent and passed it on to our own children and others we were coaching on the fine art of getting ahead. Finally, it may have become a subconscious script that sabotaged our productivity, energy, and enjoyment of quality time. For a child it was good advice and made good sense, but for adults it leads to an endless spiral of work and more work.

When we get in a heavy work cycle with numerous demands on us, typically the first thing to go is fun time. As a result, we go into a negative and unproductive spiral:

This is why it becomes absolutely essential for us to rediscover how to renew and refresh ourselves through play. This concept is not just philosophical; it is founded on hard neurological research. When you push too hard for too long and become overwhelmed, tired, and discouraged or just too tired to have much momentum, it is foolish not to seek renewal. In this state, your brain and body fill

The more we work the more tired we get the less creative or open-minded we are and the less we accomplish so we get further behind and then think we have no time for play.

DENIAL

with stress toxins and free radicals. And if you are anxious and worried about the looming mountain of work and growing pressure from deadlines, adrenaline is typically present. This brain chemical speeds up your heart rate and tenses the sphincters in the circulatory system, which moves blood away from the brain and digestion to prepare you for "fight or flight." In this state, you drop into a mental rut. You lose major blood flow to the brain, so you certainly can't do your best thinking. This is why you may not be able to remember a name or some other piece of information when you are tired, stressed, or in overload. Yet when you relax, the memory returns easily.

If your life pattern is to move from work to home, to chores, to routine with family, and back to work, you will lose your vitality and enthusiasm, perhaps so slowly that you don't notice, until one day you wake up to a life that seems mostly gray and joyless. The 100th Psalm urges: "Make a joyful noise unto the Lord, all ye lands. Serve the Lord with gladness." But too often, we serve the Lord with tiredness and seem to believe that we are doing an honorable thing. We may be so focused on our work and duty that we become joyless and humorless. Our celebration of life becomes more of an endurance contest than a sharing of our gifts with a joyful spirit.

THE SAME-O, SAME-O DISEASE

We wish we could remember the name of the minister in New Orleans who inspired us with this story. He asked: "Do you wake up in the same-o bed, next to the same-o person, put on the same-o robe to go to the same-o bathroom? Brush the same-o teeth with the same-o toothpaste? Eat the same-o breakfast in the same-o chair, drinking the same-o coffee out of the same-o cup, reading the same-o newspaper filled with the same-o bad news? Do you drive the same-o car in the same-o traffic down the same-o streets to the same-o job filled with the same-o dread?

"Do you fight the same-o battles with the same-o customers, struggling to get your work done amid the same-o interruptions and the same-o telephone demands? Attend the same-o meetings with the same-o boring agendas and finally leave to return home through the same-o traffic to the same-o family with the same-o conflicts to eat the same-o dinner and fall, exhausted, into the same-o sofa to doze off watching the same-o TV? If you do, you've got a good case of the same-o, same-o disease!"

Getting out of your rut and putting fun back in your life can make a tremendous difference in your energy and the quality of your time. We are not suggesting that you dump your spouse, buy a sports car, wear gold chains, and hang out with a new set of friends, twenty years younger than you. But climbing out of your rut, finding a new perspective on life, and becoming an open-minded, refreshed person can breathe vitality into a stale life-style or a sagging marriage.

It's interesting to learn that we don't have to (and realistical-ly can't) change others. If we only change ourselves, but we focus on healthy, meaningful changes, we will invite and inspire those around us to open up and find change in satisfying and renewing ways.

DENIAL COMPOUNDS THE PROBLEM

When we get stuck in a rut and a negative work spiral, we go into dysfunctional thinking. It goes like this:

1. We slowly forget how to play and lose our capacity to play.

2. From lack of play, we become joy-starved. Feeling neglect-

---

Denial in the "All-American Family"

Denial can apply in our work or family situations or in our perception of our role in life. Mothers who believe they must do everything for their child are denying the child's ability to do things for himself or herself while they are propping up their self-image by thinking they are essential to the child's life.

Women who see their only function in life as being a wife and mother often refuse to admit that their children have grown up and no longer need their constant attention and advice, or they may feel responsible for doing everything for their husband, including the things he could and might want to do for himself. Men who are buoyed up by thinking of their wife as an inept "little woman" deny her the opportunity for growth and themselves the freedom to make other choices.

There are many ways we can slip into denial, but the common thread is that we assume responsibilities unnecessarily and deny others the chance to be responsible for themselves. It is a heavy burden for everyone involved.

149

Imaginology: An Instant Rx for Play

Lost your ability to play? Stuck in a rut? Here are some fast, easy ways to add unexpected fun to your life.

1 Explore new territory. On a day when you are not pressed for time, drive home by a different route. You might seek a diversion like stopping by a park and feeding the ducks, walking or running, watching the sun set, admiring a tree, or taking the time to observe a detail of nature.

2 Take the little kid within you shopping and spend ten dollars or less on something you usually would not buy for yourself because it is impractical. Give yourself time to browse and find a treasure that you just want even though you know you don't need it. Enjoy your new purchase.

3 Look up an old friend from the past; call, write a letter, or visit your friend to renew contact.

4 Go someplace you have always been curious about but never explored. Here are some ideas:

A sculpture garden	An unusual restaurant	A quiet country road
A water park	The top of a high-rise building	A historic cemetery
A fire station	A tour of a storm sewer	A flea market

5 Choose an activity that you enjoy so much that you have a tendency to "get lost" in it and forget about the clock. It might be gardening, fishing, sailing, or an engaging evening with friends. Disregard the "acceptable" amount of time you "should" spend on this activity and allow yourself the freedom to enjoy yourself without time constraints.

6 Take an overnight mini-vacation on a weekend, but don't preplan, make reservations, or decide on a route. Choose an off-season time to try this without the pressure of overbooked hotels. As you travel, use your intuition and feelings to decide where to go, how long to stay, where to eat, and what to spend time on. Practice spontaneous thinking as you make your adventure happen.

7 Do something you really enjoy but haven't done since you were a kid:

Fly a kite	Carve watermelon teeth	Drag out an old musical instrument
Play hopscotch	Eat a banana split	Enter a watermelon-seed-spitting contest
Jump rope	Make a slingshot	Blow bubbles with soap or bubble gum

8 Go to a video store and rent two or three travel videos for a "Vacation Evening at Home." Pick up some ethnic take-out food on the way home to complete your evening. Who knows? It might even inspire you to call your travel agent the next day!

ed, we become rebellious, uncooperative, and even disruptive. We are at war with ourselves and others.

3. Next, we are likely to go into denial. When others encourage us to slow down or take time off, we either can't hear the message or refuse to hear it, or we feel blamed, unsupported, and unappreciated.

When we are in the denial state, we can't recognize the impact of our choices. If others suggest that we get away for a while to renew ourselves, we feel resentful at their suggestion and usually answer, "It's easy for you to say. I can't take off, I've got a critical deadline." If a spouse encourages us to spend more time at home, our response might be to feel accused of not being a good mother or father at the same time that we are working ourselves silly to provide the material things we feel our family expects and depends on us to provide.

Denial is characterized by feeling unappreciated, trapped, blamed, anxious, and without options. It's not that we don't want to slow down, but in this state, we literally don't see how we can without serious consequences. In denial, we tend to over-

exaggerate our own worth and contribution to the situation and undervalue the potential of others. We say, "I am the only one who can finish this job," believing that we don't have time to teach or coach others to help us. We continue to go for the quick fix, while we neglect long-term investments like cross-training, mentoring others, and stepping back from the urgent crisis to look for the big picture, big patterns, and creative options.

Ironically, when we are in denial, we are our own worst enemy. Even if a team or family member hands us a wonderful option that can free us from the prison of our workaholic profile, it is very likely that we will not hear the message or be able to see what is being offered; instead, it might sound more like an attack on our abilities. When others offer to help, we say to ourselves, "They're coming up with alternatives because they think I'm not doing enough and can't hack it."

TURNING IT AROUND

It seems like an overwhelming problem; how do we free ourselves from the prison of endless work and worry? Let's first look at the way a positive balance of work and play might operate during the course of a typical day:

- Early awakening; an enjoyable, brisk, aerobic walk, jog, or swim; an invigorating shower; and a healthy breakfast

- Sharing the family responsibilities of getting young children off to school; taking the time for hugs and positive anticipation of a great day

- An early arrival at work; quiet time planning your day

- Satisfying, productive work

- Joy break

- Satisfying, highly productive work

- Relaxation over mint tea or decaffeinated coffee and fruit

- Highly productive work

- Lunch break, including a brisk walk outdoors enjoying nature or a quick visit to a favorite bookstore

- A productive work session, with the ability to focus and accomplish

- Refreshing joy break

- A call to make inviting plans for the evening

- Productive work session

- Joy break with a light, nutritious snack

- Productive work

- Celebration of accomplishments at the end of a meeting; positive anticipation of rewards from joint work agreed to in the meeting

- Trip home, reviewing only the positives of the day

- At home, taking a few moments to mentally prepare for a positive time with family

When we begin to invest in this kind of positive momentum, where we blend rewarding work with time for personal refreshment and pleasure, we can accomplish far more with less effort and also enjoy a high quality of energy during the evening. Conflict is resolved with less time, stress, and strain. There also is far greater potential for creativity and teaming. When we are rested, we trust others more and they feel invited to invest their talents. Also, when people develop new talents, others are freed to follow their own pursuits.

If this all sounds too idealistic to work in the frantic, intensely demanding real world, there's a simple, easy place for us to start. The self-assessment "What's Fun for You?" will help you to discover how to get some fun back into your life.

Self-Assessment: What's Fun for You?

Take a blank sheet of paper and divide it vertically into four columns. Label each column as follows:

2–5 Minutes	5–30 Minutes	30 Minutes– ½ Day	½ Day or Longer

Now, as quickly as you can, think of what is fun for you. As each thought comes to mind, quickly enter it into the appropriate column. If shopping is fun, you would probably fit it into the third or fourth column. Fishing, golf, or a big sewing project might also fall into the longer time categories, as would special time with your significant other. Come up with as many ideas as you can in just a few minutes. When the ideas cease to flow easily and you have to ponder to come up with more, draw a line and count your results. We want you to know how many options are quickly available to you.

Next, count the number on the left side of your chart versus the right side. We have used this exercise with thousands of participants and the results follow a predictable pattern. When we are working with professionals and adults who have significant levels of responsibility, they typically run out of ideas before they get to twenty. Usually, they come up with ten to twelve ideas. Moreover, the majority of their ideas for fun require well over thirty minutes to get into and enjoy.

Why is this significant? What is your guess? We find that if our only choices for fun take long periods of time, we may become joy-starved, because few of us have half-days or longer that we feel free to devote to fun. The more joy-starved we get, the less productive we are, so it takes longer and longer to get less and less done. Also, because our productivity is down, we typically do not feel entitled to fun, so we bring work home in the evenings, work through lunch, and spend our weekends worrying about work.

Those of us who are joy-starved not only have few ideas about how to have fun quickly; we also feel we don't deserve it. When I get stuck in one of those negative all-work spirals, I subconsciously keep fun out of reach because I'm afraid if I quit working I may never start again. Sometimes I feel I don't deserve it because I'm not working well. At other times I literally can't think of anything fun to do.

JOY BREAKS—
FUN IN SMALL DOSES

How do you get off the all-work treadmill? Begin by creating and practicing two- to five-minute joy breaks several times a day. Ultimately, you want this to happen automatically without your having to remember to do it. But at the beginning, we suggest that you write these breaks into your daily plan.

It is interesting to note that when we use this self-assessment with youngsters or adults who are highly creative and productive, we find that they can fill a page of ideas, without slowing down, in two to five minutes. Look back at your own list. How many ideas do you have?

One tip that might help you expand your list of short breaks is to think of activities that are related to the longer items. For example, if "going to a movie" was on your longer list, think about adding shorter ideas to your five-minute list:

- Check the newspaper for a movie to see tonight or on the weekend.

- Call a friend and make a date for a movie.

- Read a movie review in the newspaper.

- Ask a friend to recommend a favorite movie.

Next, go to your daily schedule and begin to plan your breaks into your work day. For the first week, you might take several two- to five-minute joy breaks during the day for practice. Observe both the quality of your work and your mental processing immediately following your breaks. We think you will find a noticeable improvement in all areas.

I find that this takes constant practice, dedication, and evaluation. As I purposely begin to play using the same skills, dedication, and commitment that I bring to my work, I am amazed at the results. However, I have to keep reminding myself why I am doing this. I may be more of a workaholic than most people, but giving myself deep inner permission to play is a big hurdle for me. It helps me if I step back and assess the big-picture results and reassure myself that I am not just off on a lark. As I find that I consistently accomplish more, team more effectively, and think far more creatively when I keep my life balanced with refreshing, spontaneous play, I am able to relax and trust the process without guilt or reservation.

154

WHEN PLAY ISN'T FUN

Have you ever finished a game of golf or tennis and felt depressed or frustrated—anything but refreshed and joyful? Have you ever gone on a family outing and spent all your time keeping up with the kids and worrying about their fun, then come home exhausted? Can you re-member a vacation that became an extension of work for you? You were still rushing to meet a preplanned schedule, fitting in with other people's expectations, and going through the motions, but you were not experiencing the fun you had hoped for. What happened?

Many of us have forgotten how to play the way we did when we were children. Spend twenty

Childlike Play

1 Playing just for the fun of feeling good, not to win or for social prestige or connections.

2 Exploring and being curious just because it is enjoyable and interesting.

3 Changing focus any time your attention takes you elsewhere or you lose interest in what you are currently doing.

4 Avoiding scorekeeping or competition. Maybe you know how many chinaberries you can chunk into the birdbath, but it is just as much fun to chunk for the sake of chunking.

5 Being highly active, exploring the range of what your body can do.

6 Staying in close touch with your current emotions and feeling comfortable with spontaneous expression.

7 Using fantasy, becoming an animal, an astronaut, a villain. This allows you to explore roles and possibilities safely without it being real or permanent. (Calvin, of "Calvin and Hobbes" in the comics, is a whiz at this.)

8 Resting whenever and wherever you feel tired, staying in touch with your body's needs and responding to them.

9 Nurturing yourself and insisting that others do also. Very young children frequently get what they want because they let everyone around them know what they want and cause others to want to give it to them. We all know the symptoms when a youngster wants a nap!

minutes playing with a young child, letting the child be the leader. Notice the difference in how the child plays. There are no rules, or if there are, they change as the child's mood changes. If a rule blocks the fun, children just change the rule. Fantasy stimulates good feelings when reality seems to limit their possibilities. And there is very little competition in their play. Little children encourage each other to do well: "Let's color pictures," "Let's see if we can climb up to the highest branch," "Let's dig a hole all the way to China."

In the research for *You Don't Have to Go Home from Work Exhausted!* we learned that the mental processes used in play and creative acts actually change the chemistry of the brain and bring about more energy. Childlike play is a way to tap this resource.

Most of us have to unlearn our adult, competitive, product- and goal-oriented behavior before we can once again relax into the healing process of play. There is nothing to measure or evaluate, no score to keep—only a release of self into pleasure. Play is usually a win-win situation. And it is literally done using different mental processes. In the list at the left, we describe some of the key characteristics of childlike play. Ask yourself how recently and how often you have enjoyed this renewing kind of fun.

You can see that these characteristics of childlike play are very different from those of adult play, which focuses on competition, rules, and keeping your dignity intact. A warning! Learn the difference between *childish* and *childlike* behavior—it is critical in rediscovering the enormous fun and renewal in little-kid play.

When you are childlike, you free yourself to enjoy fun but stay aware of the needs and rights of others, making sure not to invade their privacy or become a nuisance. You don't have to play by other people's rules, but you can enjoy yourself without infringing on them. On the other hand, when you are childish, you think only of yourself and ignore the rights and feelings of others. Childish behavior will interfere with your effectiveness, while childlike behavior, in which you allow yourself to be vulnerable and trust others, can improve your effectiveness, your teamwork, and the synergy around you.

■ ■ ■ ■ ■

Ann's Game of Right-Brained Golf

My version of playing golf is very different from that of most players.

I have gotten some coaching from my patient spouse, who is a serious golfer with an eight handicap, and I learned a few basic skills such as how to chip, pitch, and putt and hit a good solid drive off a tee. But mostly I enjoy playing as though I already have the skills and know-how. If I am playing badly, I just pick up my ball and walk it up to where the others in my group hit, and I hit from there. In this way, I don't hold up my group or those behind me. And I don't suffer the humiliation of having to try to hit well with seven critical golfers watching impatiently. I don't keep score, since I usually play with rather good golfers. I play for the fun of being outdoors and sharing a sport that my husband and family enjoy.

When I get in a sand trap, I tee up the ball and hit it out effortlessly. In fact, I deftly slip a tee under my ball anytime it helps me to hit better. On a long hole, I may tee up the ball on the fairway so that I can hit it with my driver and reach the green easily.

Though I'll never play in a tournament, that's not why I play golf. I'm there for the fun of it, almost like a little child. Yet it is important for me not to obstruct or interfere with the fun of others. Oh, a few purists get bent out of shape as they realize that I am making up my own rules as I go, but as long as

157

I don't damage the course, slow down other players, or interfere with their more serious game, I don't worry.

■ ■ ■ ■ ■

NO TIME FOR PLAY? THEN MAKE TIME!

If you observe little kids, you'll see that there is no such thing as no time for play. They play at the drop of a hat. Play, for them, is not a scheduled event. It is an instant shift in attitude and perspective. They can play anywhere—jungle exploration in the doctor's office, hide-and-seek between clothes racks in a department store, or peek-a-boo over a church pew. In this same spirit, our team has explored "instant celebrations" at times when our schedule was seemingly too jam-packed for fun. Here are a few examples.

■ ■ ■ ■ ■

A Birthday Party 35,000 Feet in the Air

A few years ago, our team gave me a surprise birthday party—in the air flying on Delta from Atlanta to Dallas. We had given a big confer-

ence, and they ordered a small cake from the hotel on the way out. One of them stopped in the hotel gift shop and bought several birthday cards. There wasn't much choice and they were all pretty sappy and syrupy.

Once on board the flight my associate Jonnie Haug (a former Delta flight attendant) passed a note to the crew. As the captain welcomed the passengers, he announced my birthday and everyone on board joined in singing "Happy Birthday." Our team had secretly passed birthday invitations to the passengers who were seated close to us. The invitations read: "You are invited to a Surprise Birthday Party for Ann McGee-Cooper at 7:35 P.M. at 35,000 feet above Tuscaloosa." A birthday card was tucked into each invitation. Our neighboring passengers really got into the spirit of fun by writing ridiculous sentiments on the cards—"To a dear friend who has made these past twenty years so special," "You haven't changed since we were kids in Cincinnati. Love, Roger." Coming from complete strangers, they were a hoot!

Jonnie cut the cake and passed it all over the plane to as many passengers as we could feed. The funniest surprise was the response of the passengers. This was such a bizarre thing to do that my colleagues weren't sure how strang-

ers, mostly traveling on business, would react to such foolishness. They might have felt that it was a rude invasion of their privacy. However, just the opposite happened as everyone got into the spirit of fun and made it a jovial good time for all. Several of the passengers took their birthday invitations home because they thought it was such a great idea.

■ ■ ■ ■ ■

Spooks, Ghosts, and Goblins in the Air

Because of our business, much of our lives is spent on airplanes. After another long conference, a second memorable piece of foolishness happened on a plane. We were beat, flying home late on Halloween night. Jonnie and Kay had packed about a dozen soft rubber animal noses and several zany hats into their carry-on bags. There were crocodile and pig snouts, rabbit and mouse noses with long, white whiskers, a goat and a dog nose, a duck bill, and a chicken beak. There were also shark, giraffe, and moose heads, and one chicken hat that was totally outrageous.

Jonnie and Kay persuaded everyone sitting around us to put on something silly and just sit there

seriously to see how the flight attendants would react. They fell over themselves laughing, and the party began. The flight attendants held contests, giving away prizes they made up on the spot to the people with the oldest driver's license, a wallet or purse picture with the most people in it, and the most business cards. Then they offered free drinks to everyone "in costume."

Suddenly, people got very creative. Someone made a ghost suit by tearing two holes in a paper napkin and holding it in front of his face; others converted the barf bags into hats and animal masks. People let down their guard and made friends with strangers. When we arrived in Dallas, we were amazed at how much energy we still had even though we had been on a long flight after a three-day conference. Warm belly laughs are contagious and refreshing!

■ ■ ■ ■ ■

PLAY IS ESSENTIAL FOR GOOD TIME MANAGEMENT

Being able to play sets you free. It releases tension, washes toxins from your body, and replaces them with beneficial chemicals that rejuvenate you. Play is not a time waster; it's a time saver. Here's how it can save you time:

- Tasks don't take as long to accomplish or tire you out as quickly when you are having fun.

- A playful mind is creative and open. You will discover new solutions faster (this is a major ingredient in the area of continuous performance improvement).

- When you enjoy noncompetitive, childlike play, you trust and bond with others and respond faster to change.

- When you stop for play, you have a better, healthier, more positive attitude and will be more likely to view problems as opportunities.

- You will have a much greater possibility of enjoying good mental and physical health; as a result, you will lose less time because of illness.

- You are far more likely to admit your mistakes and profit from them. This attitude is

Celebrating Without the Calories

One of the ways our team plays together is by celebrating—we celebrate birthdays, new contract awards, product sales, bon voyages, and any other occasion we can think of. We also are a bunch of sugar-loving cookie monsters, yet we each really want to give ourselves the precious gift of good health by limiting the amount of sugar and sweets we eat. We had gotten good at celebrating and were linking play with calorie-filled goodies, so every few days we were tempted by fattening, rich sweets.

We put our creative thinking to this problem and decided to challenge ourselves to come up with healthy treats. We've had air-popped popcorn, almonds, raisins, and fresh fruit. We found an inflatable birthday cake with candles, so now we can have a fancy cake at a moment's notice without the sugar temptation. We also have put candles on a big slice of juicy watermelon in lieu of a rich dessert. Having fun with this as a team has helped each of us make better food choices, which enhances our energy long term. And how does this relate to time? How much of your time is diminished because you bottom out with sugar blues an hour or two after a gooey, sweet treat? We had no idea how much time, energy, and quality we were missing out on because we used to stay deenergized with constant sugar in our system.

essential for success in the quality movement.

- It is likely that you will be a safer, more alert worker.

In the American culture and the Protestant work ethic, we have become so focused on work and productivity that we may have lost touch with the balancing value of play, joy, and pleasant pastimes. Seeing the toll this out-of-balance life-style takes in burnout, chronic illness, and rigid thought patterns that border on denial, we realize the seductive and deceptive qualities of this shortsighted value system. If we expect to compete successfully in this time of rapid change and, even more important, to enjoy a balanced, satisfying, and rewarding life, we must get as good at creative, renewing play as we are now at highly productive work.

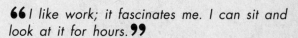

DECONTAMINATING TIME: *Reclaiming* Thirty to Sixty **FRESH HOURS** *a month*

13

> **❝** I like work; it fascinates me. I can sit and look at it for hours. **❞**
>
> —Jerome K. Jerome

> **❝** Everything becomes different when we choose to take control rather than be controlled. We experience a new sense of freedom, growth, and energy. **❞**
>
> —Dr. Eric Allenbaugh
> *Wake-Up Calls*

> **❝** You will never 'find' time for anything. If you want time, you must make it. **❞**
>
> —Charles Burton

o you ever find yourself pushing to complete that mountain of work before you only to find that the harder you push, the less you accomplish? Do you ever read to the bottom of a page only to realize that you have no idea what the page said? Or do you ever go to a movie or out for a picnic with the family and find yourself still mentally at the office—worrying about how you'll get all the work done, how the boss will react to your new idea, or how to handle a difficult customer? Maybe you finally find time to enjoy being alone with your spouse, yet your mind still replays problems at work. You want to be a responsive partner, but you are distracted by lingering worries and problems.

These are classic examples of contaminated time. We contaminate time when we are not able to stay focused in the moment, or when we are trying to do one thing, but are thinking about another. If our time is contaminated, we don't get the full benefit of either work (peak productivity) or play (total relaxation). This happens to most of us all too often.

Stop for a moment and reflect on your typical work day. How much time would you estimate gets contaminated? Consider the rest of the day—the time you spend resting, interacting with friends and family—is that time contaminated too?

Having worked with many thousands of people from all walks of life, I can report that an average of at least an hour of work time is contaminated each day because of being frazzled, tired, and distracted. Usually, toward the end of the day, our minds begin to wander, our energy drops, we've become tired, and we're ready to think of something else. All too frequently, another hour of the day is contaminated because we're too tired, too worried, or too distracted by family matters and other responsibilities to enjoy the time we have for relaxation and other fun.

We talk about work time and relaxation time, but in fact all of us have dozens of concerns in our lives: kids, parents, spouses, community issues, neighbors, friends, money, social concerns, sex, diet, health—the list goes on and on. We can't isolate everything into neat little categories, working now and forgetting everything else. It is because we have so much on our minds that it is so easy to let our time become contaminated and therefore less productive or relaxing than it could be. The first step in reversing this process is to ask yourself how much time you contaminate. The questionnaire "How Much Time Do You Contaminate?" on the next page will help you to determine this.

You may be surprised by your total. For most people, from fifteen to sixty hours a month are

How Much Time Do You Contaminate?

1 Estimate how much time you contaminate by not being totally productive during an average work day:

EXAMPLES:

- Reading the same report three times while wishing for the weekend to come
- Taking an hour to complete a twenty-minute budget draft because you are worrying about a problem with your car
- Needing to go to the supply cabinet five times to complete a travel expense report

_____

2 Now estimate how much time you contaminate on the average over the weekend or on days primarily dedicated to play, relaxation, and renewal:

EXAMPLES:

- Worrying about a client presentation while you are on the golf course
- On vacation, taking a series of business calls that spoil your mood for family fun
- Worrying about the kids and the baby-sitter while trying to enjoy an evening at the theater

_____

3 Average your work-day and weekend contamination hours and multiply by thirty (the number of days in most months). Now you have an estimate of the average total time you contaminate in a month that could be reclaimed for refreshing play or productive work:

_____

contaminated and often a great deal more! That sounds like a lot, doesn't it? It may even sound hopeless—but it's not! The good news is that you have a choice. With gentle coaching and practice, you can learn to recycle most, if not all, of that contaminated time into fresh, highly productive, rewarding, satisfying, and enjoyable new time.

DECONTAMINATING WORK TIME WITH JOY BREAKS

If you are contaminating work time, the chances are good that you need more frequent joy breaks. Most people only function at peak efficiency and total concentration for fifteen-to forty-five-minute periods, then need to break their activity with something that refreshes and invigorates them.

This can be accomplished by shifting from one kind of work to another. In a meeting, you can shift from listening to contributing, or from hearing information to making decisions. After an hour and a half, however, you may need to do something entirely different. You need time off to renew yourself. Several deep, slow breaths, a good stretch all over, a brisk walk, or a hike up and down a few flights of stairs can help to revive your body.

Your internal little kid—your right brain—needs attention, too. Just a few minutes of something fun and pleasurable can significantly restore your ability to work productively. There are a lot of simple ways for you to give yourself the break you need:

- Call a friend to make a date for lunch.

- Daydream about a recent vacation or one you'd like to take.

- Browse through a mail-order catalog to pick out future purchases.

- Enjoy a piece of fruit or a glass of cool water.

■ ■ ■ ■ ■

A Sales Manager Decontaminates Sunday Afternoons

"I was spending a Sunday afternoon having a picnic with my kids. Although it was a beautiful day and a great setting, I kept worrying about getting the house cleaned, doing the laundry, and figuring out my schedule for the coming week. Rather than spoil the whole afternoon, I decided to let the kids enjoy themselves on the playground while I got out my notebook and did some work.

"I planned when to get the household chores done and

blocked out my schedule for the week. After that was done, I began thinking that I really needed to spend some quality time with my family. It occurred to me that I could do that right now! Immediately, my mind was free to join the children and wholeheartedly enjoy the time I could spend with them.

"I find that if I check my big goals—not just the day-to-day tasks—when I get restless or worried, it helps me make clear decisions and get back on track with what's really important to me. I'm finding out that my time becomes contaminated when I behave compulsively and without thinking things through. And the more tired, burned out, and compulsive I become, the harder it is to concentrate on what is important.

"So now, as soon as I get the feeling that I'm not focused on what I'm doing, I take a moment to evaluate what is going on—and make the necessary adjustments."

■ ■ ■ ■ ■

The Five-Minute Rule

Marilynn Williamson, executive vice president of Drake Beam Morin, Inc., says:

"It's so simple, but it makes all the difference. In my family we have created a tradition in which we devote the first five minutes of our evening exclusively to each

other. The idea came from a comment a colleague made one day. She noted that the early part of an interview often sets the tone. Within the first few minutes, she could tell whether the candidate would work out or the client would buy into her idea.

"It occurred to me that I might not be using my first few minutes at home in the evening in the best way. When I get home after a busy day at the office, I am often in overdrive. How many times have I set the tone for the evening by being too busy to give my husband and family the attention they deserve? Now, we take time to sit down, listen, and totally af-

firm each other. It's amazing the effect it has."

. . . . .

LEARN TO PAY ATTENTION TO YOUR THREE-YEAR-OLD

When we become joy-starved, our right brain begins to interrupt our concentration much as a three-year-old child might. Our mind becomes distracted and wanders, going off on tangents when we're trying to concentrate. It's like a kid pulling on your pant

leg begging for attention; the longer you ignore the tugging, the more insistent it becomes. If we get annoyed with ourselves and try to push longer and harder, the problem only becomes worse, as the kid becomes cranky and rebellious. Isn't that how you feel inside when you try to force yourself to stay focused past your level of highest productivity?

Test this strategy: Spend a week noticing when your productivity begins to drop. Look back at your list of two- to five-minute joy breaks from Chapter Twelve. When you feel your productivity beginning to drop, select an item from your list and shift into a joy break. Now go back to work. Keep this rotation of work and play going, and then estimate the results. We think you will be amazed to discover that with a few well-spaced joy breaks all through your work day, you can significantly increase your productivity and the amount of highly focused work time you enjoy.

The significant word here is *enjoy*. Isn't work far more satisfying when you are accomplishing at a high level? Isn't the biggest part of the mental and physical drain you experience from work happening because you get far too tired before you take a rest or joy break? Instead of taking time to scold yourself for not wanting to continue work, spend that time having a minute of fun.

Professionals who have learned the benefits of decontaminating with joy breaks create ways to support one another. Mary Jane Brown, managing director of Walnut Creek Drake Beam Morin, Inc., in San Jose, California, explains:

"The Walnut Creek Drake Beam Morin 'buddy system' provides an opportunity to take a joy break, feel good, and make someone else feel good—all at the same time! Every three months, the entire office staff draws the name of a fellow staff member. Buddies are not reciprocal.

"The system was put in place a couple of years ago to provide a fun way to make at least one other person (your buddy) feel special in a variety of ways—a surprise flower, café latte, a breakfast goodie, a lunch, a cartoon, or anything to make someone know he or she was thought of."

DECONTAMINATING PLAYTIME BY LETTING GO OF GUILT

If you are contaminating playtime, there are two issues to consider. Do you value your play for its own sake— experiencing and sharing fun, joy, and downtime as a necessary and valuable dimension of life? And do you give yourself unconditional permission to frequently enjoy free play?

Sometimes we simply need to unlearn our polarized belief that only work is important and realize that without refreshing, renewing play, we lower our capacity for high-quality work and our ability to enjoy life fully. Also, without refreshing, joyful play, our life can lose all of its enthusiasm. Constant work unbalances our immune system. Doctors who were surveyed in an American Medical Association poll believed that anywhere from 65 to 75 percent of illnesses occurring prior to the age of sixty-five are made more severe by unrelieved exposure to distress.

Most of us will never "finish" everything we could possibly do. Responsible adults generate work simply by working, so if we insist on finishing all our work before we can play, we'll never get to play. Play needs to be seen as a balancing resource that is as necessary to retaining our mental and physical health as are regular, nutritious meals, stimulating exercise, and enough rest.

DECONTAMINATING PLAYTIME BY GETTING BACK TO WORK

At times, however, our guilt is an appropriate inner warning that we have made commitments to ourselves and others that we are not honoring. Perhaps we have been playing long enough, and now it is time to return to work. Only you will know what fits your situation and when you need to either turn off inappropriate guilt or heed a legitimate warning.

■ ■ ■ ■ ■

A Corporate Executive Learns to Be Present with His Family

"I spent years working long hours, really believing that I was doing what a loving, responsible father and parent should do. I often felt torn because most nights I was attending a community function or client dinner and most weekends I had a briefcase full of paperwork to consume me. Somehow, I believed that one day it would be different—that I would get all the work done—but it never was.

"Now my children are grown. There are no more soccer games to coach or attend. No one is waiting,

The Peace Pilgrim

In the last decade, a woman in her seventies known only as The Peace Pilgrim walked across America, spreading her own spirit of love and tranquility. This list describes the inner changes she experienced as she gained a new and broader perspective on life.

1 A tendency to think and act spontaneously rather than from fears based on past experiences

2 An unmistakable ability to enjoy each moment

3 A loss of interest in judging oneself

4 A loss of interest in judging others

5 A loss of interest in conflict

6 A loss of interest in interpreting the actions of others

7 A loss of ability to worry

8 Frequent, overwhelming episodes of appreciation

9 Contented feelings of connectedness with others and nature

10 Frequent attacks of smiling through the eyes of the heart

11 Increasing susceptibility to love extended by others as well as the uncontrollable urge to extend it

12 An increasing tendency to let things happen rather than to make them happen

hoping that I will get home in time to shoot a few baskets. And my memories are more about the special times I missed than the special times that I shared with my kids. I missed moments I can never recover. I regret that I didn't weave more time for my kids and my wife into my work schedule. What I didn't enjoy then, I can never reclaim. I only hope others can learn from my story.

"Learning about contaminating time helps me understand the negative spiral I created for myself. When my family resented my absence, I felt unappreciated and hurt. I thought that what mattered the most were the money I earned and the benefits it brought. My now-grown children tell me they would rather have had a father.

"I have been practicing decontaminating time now for about two years. I can tell you that my marriage is totally renewed. We now enjoy and look forward to evenings of fun and shared feelings and thoughts, and each of us feels deeply in love once more. And now that I am learning to be totally present in whatever I am doing, even my grown children are becoming far closer and more loving. I think they have learned a valuable lesson from my misplaced priorities. And they have chosen to forgive me and understand my confusion and faults. My mistake was

to think only about the present challenge instead of about long-term goals.

"I have seen so many companies furlough middle managers who gave their total dedication to the company for their entire careers. The bitterness of having given up precious family time for years only to be put out to pasture has been more than many of them can deal with. I hope I can be a role model for living in balance and encouraging all our employees to create a healthy balance in their lives. Strong, happy, healthy families are a tremendous asset for corporations. This is a resource not to be taken for granted—and an issue we've ignored too long. I intend to change this for myself and my company!"

DECONTAMINATING TIME THROUGH BALANCE

Balancing different life activities is the key to peak performance. Examine your time and how you spend (or contaminate) it. Remember that balance doesn't mean a simplistic fifty-fifty split of work and play. The division might be five to ninety-five in a situation where you need to concentrate or focus with a time deadline, or it might be seventy to thirty when you are relaxing with the kids but still need to be wearing your parenting hat. And it changes daily or hourly. Balance is whatever is necessary to keep your life at optimal performance at any given moment:

- Sometimes you may need to get away and enjoy time alone.

- You may need to find help in accomplishing a task rather than trying to do everything yourself.

- At times, you may need a ten-minute nap or a vigorous round with a jump rope.

- And sometimes you may need to go ahead and finish a specific onerous task and get it out of the way.

You must decide how to balance your life, for only you can see the big picture. Only you know what your commitments and goals are and can hear your inner voice. Learn to listen to your body and trust it. When you get restless, have on hand creative ways to rest, delight, and renew yourself.

When you are working too hard, your body tells you to slow down and take a break. The same is true of play. If you are playing and get restless and distracted by thoughts of work, your sub-

---

Barbara McCroby, lecturer on whole-brained thinking and holistic healing, helps to create national advertising campaigns as a partner in Abbott Advertising. She describes herself as a "half century old homemaker" and talks about how with age has come a perspective she never had as a young person.

"Everything that I had experienced during those first fifty years began to pay off like interest on an investment . . . only it was in something that money can't buy. The pay-off was in feelings . . . emotions . . . deep love and appreciation for life and a desire to work harder making each year one of growth. . . .

"With each passing year I notice changes in me. . . .

"I may be doing less each day, but I'm doing more worthwhile things. Eliminating the unnecessary chatter of a too-busy life can make your days full to the brim!"

conscious may be telling you that it's time to get back to work. By trying to keep the big picture in mind, you will see that work and play are both essentials of a balanced, fulfilling life. Then, when you are trying to have fun but keep thinking of work, you can work or plan for a while and again release your capacity to play.

As you enjoy more family and personal time, you will bring more productive energy, much clearer and more creative thinking, and a better attitude to everything you do. You will become a better listener and will be less likely to become grumpy, preoccupied, or impatient. Unhappiness is often the result of burnout that happens when we constantly contaminate both our work time and our playtime.

Learning to create a system with which to see your life, not as a series of notes to be played, but as a symphony to be harmonized, will help you find more time and deeper enjoyment of the time you have.

COMPOUNDING TIME: CREATING *more* TIME WHEN YOU NEED IT

66 Now that I had 'run out of time,' I seemed to have more time than ever before. 99

—Dr. Paul Pearsall
discussing diagnosis of his cancer,
in *Making Miracles*

66 The great pleasure in life is doing what people say you cannot do. 99

—Walter Bagehot

66 Too much of a good thing can be wonderful. 99

—Mae West

few years after I had
started my own company, I began
to struggle with the same problem
other entrepreneurs confront—
how to get everything done that was
put before me and still have some time
for renewal. As our business grew, so did
the demands. There were books to write,
manuscripts to edit, phone calls and interviews to answer, reading to digest, speaking en-
gagements to fulfill, and nine associates on our

own team who needed daily time with me. Not only did the workload seem overwhelming and undoable, the chances that I would be able to find time for myself seemed impossible.

It was depressing to think I would never have time again to paint, garden, take tap-dancing lessons, swim, or pursue other pleasures I missed or wished for. To complicate the problem even further, more and more of my time was being spent in taxis, on planes, waiting at airports, and standing in hotel check-in lines— the inconveniences those of us who travel so often face.

As I observed other people in the same circumstances, I began to notice that some people led extremely busy and productive lives and still found time for the activities they loved and the habits that kept them healthy and balanced! I also noticed that one of the patterns that seemed to run true in highly creative people, peak performers, and those thought of as geniuses was that they led full, productive lives and enjoyed many passions and interests while achieving the seemingly impossible.

Think of people such as Pablo Picasso, who created an incredible number of works of art well into his nineties; Margaret Mead, who wrote books and was ac-

tive into her seventies; Albert Schweitzer; Georgia O'Keeffe; Thomas Edison; Thomas Jefferson; and Buckminister Fuller, who was an inventor, futurist, writer, and architect. Herb Kelleher of Southwest Airlines Company and most other successful CEOs also match this pattern and as a result are typically productive and creative well into their later years. What is the secret of these people?

ACCOMPLISHING MORE THAN ONE GOAL AT A TIME

While most people live as though time were linear, highly successful, productive people use a concept called *com-*

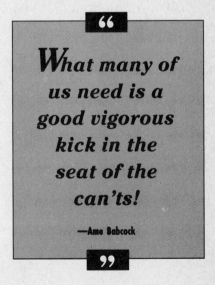

What many of us need is a good vigorous kick in the seat of the can'ts!

—Ame Babcock

Things I'd Like to Do . . .
but NEVER Get Around to!

Make a list of all the things you'd really like to do, to enjoy, to accomplish—things that you never seem to get around to. Here are some suggestions to get you started:

- Spend quality time with friends and family.
- Enjoy classical or other favorite music.
- Read or write poetry.
- Exercise regularly.
- Develop better listening skills.
- Write letters to your extended family and friends.
- Do household chores, such as spring cleaning.
- Learn to play a musical instrument.
- Plant a vegetable garden.

- Learn a new sport.
- Improve your positive conflict-resolution skills.
- Sing in a chorus.
- Join a community action group.
- Ride a horse.
- Take windsurfing lessons.
- Learn a foreign language.
- Kayak in white water.

pounding. For you to understand compound time, it will be helpful to first do the exercise at the top of this page. After you have completed it, consider how you schedule your day and your week. Do you think in linear time—one activity for each time period—as shown below?

6:00 A.M.   Wake up, eat breakfast, dress

7:00 A.M.   Commute to work

8:00 A.M.   Staff meeting

9:00 A.M.   Appointment with Jane Smith to resolve problem

1:00 P.M.   Lunch with client

Get out your most recent calendar and review your past week. Was it scheduled in linear time?

Now let's think in compound time, which provides opportunities to accomplish more than one goal within the same amount of time. Look at these same events, only this time with additional activities blended to gain the advantages of compounding time.

The strategy is easy. Find times when you already have an activity scheduled but when you think you might be able to accomplish something else at the same time. Look back at your wish list. What items could you combine with activities that are already on your calendar? Could you learn a foreign language from tapes while commuting to work? Could you spend quality time with your kids by taking horseback riding lessons with them instead of sitting around the house together on Saturday morning watching cartoons?

Here are some of our favorite examples of compounding by people who get a lot accomplished and still enjoy balanced, happy, productive lives:

■ Get up an hour earlier to enjoy aerobic exercise and listen to a favorite tape while running or walking.

■ Do positive mental imaging while you are dressing for work. Visualize yourself performing at the highest level of excellence.

■ While driving to work, listen to taped transcripts of meetings you weren't able to attend.

■ Practice active listening skills in a regularly scheduled staff meeting. Pass out seminar materials to your team and let them in on what you are doing. Invite their support and participation.

■ Walk a meeting with a colleague. You think better if you walk briskly, and you can both use the fresh air and exercise. Stop to enjoy a piece of fresh fruit and a big glass of water, while you resolve your differences and turn problems into opportunities.

■ Call your spouse from work. Plan something fun for the evening or weekend.

6:00 A.M.	7:00 A.M.	8:00 A.M.	9:00 A.M.	1:00 P.M.
Wake up, eat breakfast, dress	Commute to work	Staff meeting	Appointment with Jane Smith to resolve problem	Lunch with client
Listen to favorite music	Learn Spanish on audiocassettes	Practice mind-mapping	Share leadership idea	Plan a time to play racquetball
		Practice stress-reduction techniques	Practice conflict-resolution skills	Practice listening techniques

- Learn the technique of *mind-mapping* from Tony Buzan's book, *Use Both Sides of Your Brain*. Mind-mapping builds your memory and keeps all your complex information on one page. Then, mind-map your next speech, report, or meeting agenda.

- At lunchtime, make a quick stop at a bookstore or magazine stand to browse current reading of interest in the career section and then check out the vacation, hobby, and special-interest sections. Choose something that looks like it would be fun to learn.

- Practice win-win-win negotiation skills in a meeting. Bring a one-page sheet of guidelines and invite an outside facilitator to keep the group search-

ing for mutual solutions rather than moving quickly to win-lose options. Invite the facilitator to debrief and coach the group after the meeting so that you can continue to improve. Celebrate any progress; don't wait to get perfect.

- On the commute home, think only about what you did well that day. Celebrate your accomplishments.

- Enjoy a brisk game of basketball with a teenager (great aerobics!) and then prepare dinner together. Enjoy sharing conversation about each other's day. Offer something from your day that might have been seen as a failure and tell what you learned from it. This helps your youngster see mistakes as learning opportunities, and not something to run from.

Southwest Airlines Company provides a positive demonstration of compounding in business.

In 1991, Southwest reported 2,267 passengers per employee. In 1993, this had grown to 2,698 passengers per employee. The carrier that had the closest ratio was America West, with 1,462 passengers per employee.

This means that Southwest had to find creative ways for each person to accomplish the productivity of two or more! The employees did this by combining more than one goal within one time frame or partnering with oth-

Great Compounding Ideas for Those with Heavy Travel Schedules

Advances in technology allow entire new vistas for compounding. Dave Wilson, national director of professional development, Ernst & Young, travels with his laptop computer and drafts correspondence while traveling. At night, he dials up the mailbox of his secretary, Diane Spearman, and (1) retrieves all of his messages, (2) leaves messages for his colleagues, and (3) sends his draft correspondence for polishing. Then, when he returns, his letters are all completed, edited, spell-checked, formatted, and waiting for his signature.

On longer trips, his secretary uses Federal Express to send all correspondence to him to sign and return. He carries Federal Express envelopes with him, preaddressed and billed to his office. With each package his secretary sends him, she includes another return envelope.

183

Creating Time with Corporate Compounding

While Caroline Ewing was working with Les McCraw, who was then president and CEO of Fluor Daniel, Les was frequently out of the office traveling. Caroline would draft a brief page of bullets noting the events of the day so that when he returned to the office, he was kept abreast of events that might color his work and decisions in the days to come. Caroline made a habit of thinking of the big picture and searching out ways to preplan or suggest options that would create two benefits within the same time period.

On one of Les's trips, Carolyn noted that I was returning to Dallas on a commercial flight the same afternoon that Les was flying to Dallas on the company plane to work with clients. Her suggestion that I fly on the company plane gave us two hours to confer about what had happened with my recent work (and saved their company the cost of an airline ticket). Gerald Glenn, then vice president of marketing, was also along. As a result of Caroline's going the extra mile, the three of us gained the benefit of a two-hour-plus creative brainstorming session that otherwise would never have happened.

ers to extend time and productivity. Here are some examples:

- At gate turnarounds, flight attendants, pilots, and station personnel double as cleanup crews and quickly clean the cabins. They have record fifteen-minute turnarounds. And it's not unusual to see pilots loading passengers' baggage, pushing wheelchairs, or cleaning the cabin.

- What they call Southwest Spirit is expressed in many ways. Recently, two off-duty flight attendants were flying on a full flight. Typically flights are short, so after takeoff they got up and helped pass out peanuts and take drink orders. When they were asked why they would go to work when they were off duty, they answered, "Well, it's a full flight and we couldn't *not* do it. It would be much harder to stay in our seats than to join in providing the great service we want to be remembered for!"

- One year, off-duty employees got together and took Christmas dinner to the operational teams scheduled to work on Christmas Day. They said, "We want them to feel appreciated. Besides, part of Christmas is giving and sharing love."

Most people would call this working overtime. Southwest calls it having fun and letting others know they are appreciated.

CREATING BALANCE

Warning! As you become really good at compounding, you may find that you begin to overdo it. You may get almost compulsive and feel that you aren't being productive unless you are compounding every minute of every hour. Remember the importance of balance. It is just as important to have some time that is open, unscheduled, unrushed, and spontaneous— even "do nothing" time—as it is to be highly efficient at compounding:

- Spend at least twenty minutes enjoying something fun and special each evening, such as planning when and how you can get started on a new hobby.

- Do absolutely nothing for five minutes. Relax. Let all the tension drain from your body.

Empty your mind of all cares and thoughts.

- Remember to enjoy special time with your life partner. Relax and just enjoy being nurturing, playful, and loving with each other and totally present for each other's needs.

Others will sense it if you become compulsive about efficiency, and they will feel discounted. For example, if you tell your teenaged daughter, "Okay, we have thirty minutes to have fun, play basketball, and discuss our day, so start talking!" she might feel like just one more item on your busy agenda, rather than someone you really want to be with.

So enjoy creating balance. In the process, have some fun building several new hours into every twenty-four. We have found we can live more than one lifetime at once. And as we study highly effective, creative people, we discover that they are masters at creative compounding, which contributes to their higher goals in life.

saying NO *as* EASILY AS YOU SAY *yes*

15

❝Frankly, my dear, I don't give a damn.❞

—Rhett Butler to Scarlett O'Hara in *Gone with the Wind*

❝Don't let your mouth write a check your body can't cash.❞

—Flip Wilson
as Geraldine

❝I am humbled by my realization of the sacredness of the time we are given and stunned by our irreverence for the time we have.❞

—Dr. Paul Pearsall
Making Miracles

Many of us who are divergent thinkers have spent a great deal of time on projects we didn't care about because we didn't know how to say no to others or to our own sense of duty. At other times, we have really cared about the cause or believed that our abilities were needed, but we failed to recognize one important fact: we can't be on every committee or task force, attend every meeting that we are "needed" for, or accept every assignment because we are "the only one who can pull it off." As our team has talked to several thousand creative people over the past dozen years, we have seen this as a classic time management problem.

GOOD LITTLE GIRLS AND BOYS DON'T SAY NO

There are many reasons why people hesitate to say no to a request for their time or energy. In addition to our individual personality traits, we all receive strong cultural messages as we are growing up. At birth we are helpless and dependent on others to make our decisions, love us, and protect us. As we grow into children, we still are expected to do as we are told; our parents decide what we will do and when we will do it. As two-year-olds, we love to say "No!" We learn the word, but we also learn that it belongs to someone else. Good little girls and good little boys don't say no when they are told to do something.

Furthermore, we are taught that being agreeable is a positive trait. If we say no to people, we will hurt their feelings, and they may not like us anymore. This is the basis of the peer pressure that gets so many young people (and adults) into trouble. When we say yes, we are rewarded with friendship (or what seems like friendship), approval, and smiles. When we say no, we may experience punishment, rejection, frowns, and even ridicule.

Regrettably, no clear line is drawn between childhood and maturity. No one says to us, "Okay, forget all those things you learned when you were little to keep you safe. You don't need them anymore. Here are the new rules." Instead, we keep those old feelings deep inside and revert to childhood fears whenever we want to say no: "What if they don't ask me again? What if they hate me? What if they won't be my friend anymore? What if I become unlovable and unprotected?"

Once we reach a certain level of maturity, we begin making decisions for ourselves. Teenagers practice saying no to their parents all the time, but it is very difficult for them to refuse their friends' requests. This same kind of dichotomy appears later in life as well. We sometimes find it difficult to say no to supervisors when they ask us to do impossible feats. It is part of our early training not to talk back to our parents. After all, the authority

A Place to Begin
PRACTICE SAYING NO

Get a friend to role play situations involving an abusive salesperson. Together you can brainstorm possible responses and practice until you are comfortable with them. Practice prepares us for real situations and helps us to reprogram our initial inner responses. It also gives us time and space to understand what is going on behind the scenes—to see which buttons the salesperson is trying to push.

You know the routine. The salesperson asks, "What will it take for you to buy this car right now?" You have several choices, one of which is to say politely and firmly, "I am not going to buy this car right now, but I would like to know what you are offering and after I have considered your deal, I'll be glad to let you know my decision."

figure has always decided what will be done. Our peers and co-workers also ask for help and time; after hours, friends, family, and community leaders make demands. These constant requests can be overwhelming.

SELF-ESTEEM AND SAYING NO

There is a connection between how we feel about our-

selves and others and our ability to say no. If we feel confident, secure, and valued, it is easier to weigh the merits of a request and respond calmly. If we feel inferior, powerless, and undervalued, we think we have no choices; we respond to the request by saying yes even when we want to say no, or we say no in an emotional and defensive manner.

If we recognize that we are an important part of a business team and others acknowledge our value to the team effort, it becomes much easier to say, "No, I can't take on that part of the project right now because it will endanger another part that I am committed to finish first." We are confident that our judgment is correct and that our partners will understand the situation.

On the other hand, if our work is constantly denigrated, minimized, and ignored, we will be more inclined to respond by saying yes in the hope that maybe this one heroic effort will win our partners over. Or we might say, "No, damn it! I already have more than my share of this project and the rest of you are just sitting on your hands!"

We are all aware of these regressive dynamics on one level or another. All of us have been battered by salespeople who play on our insecurity and uncertainty: "Is this too expensive for you?" "Do you have to ask your wife before you can buy something?" "Honey, let me explain this to you again." They are playing on our fear of appearing powerless, inadequate, or indecisive. Others may try to enlist our sympathy by telling us they have to sell just one more vacuum cleaner, car, or magazine subscription to make their quota and buy the baby some shoes. They need our understanding, need our help, need us. We are taught to be caring, helping people, so it is very hard to say no—besides, they won't like us anymore if we don't help out. The fact is that we hurt ourselves and reinforce their

Become aware that saying yes to someone else is usually an automatic no to something you had planned for yourself.

negative and manipulative behavior when we submit to this type of treatment.

THE STIGMA OF SAYING NO IN BUSINESS

In today's world of business, "Superb Quality" and "Outstanding Customer Service" are no longer just slogans; they have become necessities for any business that is going to survive in this decade of high competition. With the quality and customer-service movements have also come some interesting phrases like "The customer is always right," "No is not in our company vocabulary," and "We always will find a way to meet your request."

Divergent, creative people are masters at brainstorming all the ways to get something done in what seem like impossible situations. The business philosophy of never saying no to a client or customer is fuel for the right-brained, divergent mind. It fires us up to promise anything. Now we not only have the internal motivation of tackling the impossible challenge; we also have the admonition of business. We "have to" say yes. If we say no, we'll find ourselves out of business.

There is some faulty logic at work here. Since we have only a finite amount of time to work on projects, supply services, and deliver products, if we don't say no to any requests, some of our clients are going to suffer down the line. A short suit of those of us who are divergent is imagining in advance how taking on one more project will affect all of our other commitments on the schedule, especially those that are not already in progress. When the hours or days run out, a natural prioritizing will occur. We will have to say no to somebody, and it probably won't be the one we would have chosen at the beginning of the cycle.

The old saying "If you want something done, find a busy person" hooks into the profile we have been describing. We divergent people thrive on having lots of irons in the fire and one more just makes the challenge more interesting . . . to a point.

ible consequences of saying yes until it is too late. When I say yes to one more worthy cause, that means something else has to give. Frequently, what I lose is personal time, time with Larry, the opportunity to communicate with my team so they know what they need to do, and time for other duties that are important but not urgent. It took me a long time to realize that when I overcommit myself, I penalize not just myself but all those around me as well. Typically, I used to get ill as a result of taking on too much for too long on all fronts. Isn't it interesting that illness can become a way in itself of saying no? Unfortunately, it severely limits everyone's options. It is important to become aware that saying yes to someone else is usually an

THE INVISIBLE CONSEQUENCES OF SAYING YES

Learning to see the downside of this tendency has been a great opportunity for me. My spouse, Larry, and my business partner, Duane, have been patient teachers. My tendency is to fail to recognize all the invis-

automatic no to something you had planned for yourself.

STRATEGIES TO HELP YOU LEARN TO SAY NO

What is the solution? In my case, it helped me to first get a better understanding of the causes of the problem. I enjoy being needed and contributing to others, so when I was asked for help, it was always satisfying to say yes. I couldn't see the results of my accepting yet another invitation until it was too late. I encourage you to ask yourself if you are the sort of person I have been describing. You may or may not be.

Next, our team experimented with some strategies that we developed for divergent people to help them in learning to say no. Use them as a way to untangle your own pattern of getting caught in this type of situation.

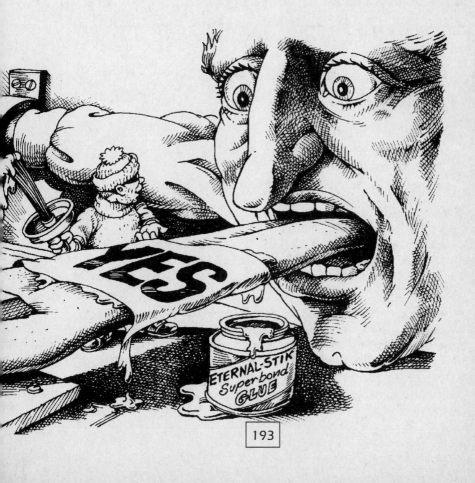

Block Out the Entire Commitment on Your Calendar

Remember, those of us who are right-brain-dominant are visual. Until we "see it," a request to serve as program chairperson for the professional conference is just an abstraction. It sounds like a great thing to do. The conference certainly could use some fresh, creative ideas, and it probably will just take a short brainstorming meeting of maybe, at most, a half-day. Wrong!

If someone calls and asks you to take on another project, don't say yes or no until you have had some time to think through the total time commitment and block it out on your calendar. If you have done the task before, list the

---

10 Things I Could Do . . .
if I Didn't Give My Time Away

If many of your requests for help come to you by telephone, make a list of at least ten things you really would like to enjoy or accomplish that keep getting pushed to the back burner. Here are some we typically postpone:

- Enjoying a leisurely lunch with a special friend
- Spending a romantic weekend with our spouse
- Reading a good book
- Swimming three times a week to improve our health
- Gardening
- Enjoying some quality one-on-one time with our children

Post this list by the phone and take time to review it before saying yes to someone else's worthy cause. Better yet, ask for twenty-four hours to consider the request. In the meantime, consult your mate or invite other objective input on the pros and cons of the invitation. Then practice graceful ways to decline.

When you successfully decline, reward yourself by claiming one of the wished-for items on the list. When you cave in to yet another enticing plea for help, mark off an item on your list to raise your awareness of what that yes to others means to you. Be aware that some valid requests will come your way in the midst of this exercise. If you decide the request is worthy of your time and effort, go for it, but mark off an item to remind you of the tradeoff you just made.

steps, estimate the amount of time they will take (it's usually a safe bet to double or even triple the amount of time that you first estimate), and put the steps on Post-it Notes on your calendar. If you can find a place for them and it looks reasonable, you can feel good about accepting. If your calendar is already very full, the physical, visual act of trying to find a space for these parts of the task will help you to honestly say no.

What if you have never done the task or assignment and don't know what kind of time commitment it involves? It is critical that you buy some time in these situations before answering. Call people who had these same responsibilities in the past and get them to talk you through the different tasks, including how long it took them and how long they think it will take you (a novice) to do the same job. Does it appear to require a lot of time and effort up front? Believe me, it is nothing compared to the time commitment of a request you have agreed to without knowing what is involved.

Now my calendar serves as a visual tool I use to see in advance what another yes will mean. On it I color-code travel, presentations, big projects, writing, fun time, family time, social commit-

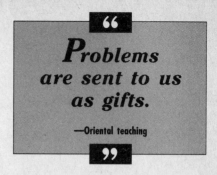

> **Problems are sent to us as gifts.**
>
> —Oriental teaching

ments, and so forth. Next I block in all the preparation time each item requires, such as in-town travel, rehearsals, telephone calls, exercise, and shopping. I even add my personal time in advance so there will be something there for me. Because I am a highly visual person, this system keeps me aware of when I have balance or when I am becoming overcommitted.

Get a Second Opinion

As a special personal tool, because I know that I am especially vulnerable to a good cause, I have made a commitment to myself, my family, and my business team not to accept or book a commitment without first discussing it with one of the people who will be affected. They don't tell me what to do, but they do help me to realize the variables of my decisions.

I am amazed that even after years of practice, I still need time

Involve Talented People Who Have Been Forgotten

Make and keep a list of people with talents who are underused. For example, retired people, students, newcomers to town, young people, and physically challenged people may all have talents and capabilities that they would love to share but that for a variety of reasons are being overlooked.

If you keep this list handy, you can refer the person to whom you must say no to someone else who might welcome the opportunity to help out. During the twenty years I have kept my list, I have been able to get several young people started in business and have involved many gifted and special people in projects they were pleased to support. Sometimes I served as a mentor during the planning stages to help them realize that they did have the necessary skills. I frequently learned that they performed far more effectively than I would have if I had said yes and then struggled to juggle this new commitment with an already overcrowded schedule.

It is fun to network and enjoy balance at the same time. Just be sure you play fair. It isn't fair to make a referral unless you are reasonably sure the person you are recommending is qualified and will welcome the call. Don't pass on your problems unless you believe you are doing both people a favor.

to weigh the outcomes of my decisions. In the moment, I still tend to say yes and then find a way to make it happen—even if it comes out of my hide, sleep, and well-being. I now realize that this is a very half-brained approach! By using only my right-brain thinking skills that love people (and fear rejection) and not balancing them with some left-brain thinking skills that can analyze the time I will need and any hidden negatives that may result, I can't come up with the best answer.

One of my gifts, to care deeply about others and enjoy serving, is overplayed into a weakness when I respond to every request by saying yes. To balance this gift, I consult the opposite gifts of my partners to see the downside of these opportunities, asking them to play the devil's advocate. Together we have learned to make much better decisions for all parties, consulting and respecting everyone and making them part of the process that will ultimately affect all of us.

Rehearse Saying No Graciously, Thoughtfully, and Firmly

One of the main reasons we can't say no is because we don't know how. My team has begun to collect and become aware of gracious but firm ways to decline and has learned a lot by simply observing friends and colleagues who have polished this skill. When I was struggling so hard to allow myself to say no, I began to realize that some of my favorite people could do this so graciously that I felt fine no matter whether their answer was yes or no. What made the difference?

Typically those people were comfortable with themselves and so firmly committed to their own personal goals that they clearly affirmed me and my invitation while letting me know why they did not choose to help. For example, a colleague said:

"Thank you for giving me the opportunity to consider helping out with the bake sale. I do appreciate the invitation, but all of my time is committed during this month, and I am very careful to respect my limits. Thank you for understanding."

Another gracious response to a social invitation went like this:

"Thank you for the invitation. I would really enjoy an evening in your home, and your dinners are always delicious. However, I have plans for that evening. Please accept my regrets."

Yet another colleague handled pressure in a positive way that earned my respect. When the other person wouldn't take no for an answer, my friend calmly but firmly responded:

"You obviously have a strong commitment to find good people to join you in this project. I have an equally strong commitment to keep this weekend open for family time. I am trusting you to understand our differences on this and my decision to decline."

We encourage you to notice how people whom you admire decline in ways that don't leave you or others feeling discounted or rejected. These responses affirm your intent and interest *and* their conflicting but equally significant purpose or need. To affirm both without putting one over the other is balance.

Warning: Be careful about saying "Maybe." One way many people avoid saying yes or no is by postponing a decision. This simply postpones the problem as well. If you say "Maybe," you're not playing fair with yourself or others. Don't suggest a possibility unless your intent is genuine. Saying "Maybe next time" makes the task of saying no even harder the next time because you feel you have already partially committed yourself.

197

CREATING "THIRD RIGHT ANSWERS"

Now that we've given you lots of support and encouragement to expand your skills in setting limits with others, know that balance is still the key. Life is too complicated for one approach or set of skills to always work. Let me explain this further.

At work, it often isn't enough to just say no. It may solve your immediate problem, but it may also block a team member who is working toward shared goals. Someone has to get "it" done. If we feel overwhelmed and come out with a firm *"No!"* we are reacting to a part of the problem and

> *The purpose of learning to say no is to give yourself control over your own time.*

not reflecting on all the related parts. The question should be: "How can we create, together, a reasonable way for all the goals to get met without overloading anyone or reneging on an essential promise?"

We use the term *third right answer* to signal a call for keeping the discussion open. Your position is to want me to say yes to your request. My position is that I need to say no to protect myself from becoming overloaded. Could there be a third alternative that neither one of us is seeing now? Perhaps I can help you to get started, or help you to find another resource, or get an extension so that I can work on it next week.

Bonnie McElearney, manager of personnel development for the City of Dallas, explains:

"In city government, many times you find yourself working with inflexible people in an inflexible system. The key to getting things done is building relationships in advance so that when you have needs, you can get the resources and personal support you desire. Start with personal needs. Sell others on the benefits of a project in terms of their needs. If you get a no, try partnering. Say, 'If I can do this with you, could you complete it or take it the next step forward?' "

SAYING YES WITH CONFIDENCE

The purpose of learning to say no is to give yourself control over your own time. The more you value yourself and the more valuable you are to others, the more important it becomes for you to have the skill and confidence to say no without cutting off the relationship.

Your yeses will become more fun and more satisfying if they are freely given. When they are no longer contaminated by too many commitments, when they are not the result of arm twisting, and when they are the result of making a positive decision rather than avoiding a negative decision, you can say yes wholeheartedly, and you will be able to say no in a way that you feel good about and that your listener will hear and be able to accept.

EXECUTIVE
neglect:
NEVER GET AROUND TO *some* STUFF!

16

> 66 Practice not-doing and everything will fall into place. 99
>
> —Lao Tzu, *Tao Te Ching*

> 66 Tell me what you pay attention to and I will tell you who you are. 99
>
> —José Ortega y Gasset

> 66 My husband and I have figured out a really good system about the housework: neither one of us does it. 99
>
> —Dottie Archibald

When I first became an administrator, a close friend gave me the gift of executive neglect. He wisely said, "You are an executive when you are responsible for more than you can personally accomplish. Learn to let go of some of it. You will become consumed if you expect to do it all!" As dependent children and dependent workers, our job was to do as we were told and do all of it.

But as thoughtful, creative, interdependent leaders, we realize that it is just as important to know what *not* to do as it is to get work done. The ability to weigh fast-changing priorities is essential to success and survival.

Just using the term *executive neglect* has helped me over the years. When I am overwhelmed, I often ask, "Where can I apply executive neglect?" A key to being a successful leader is to learn what is safe to neglect. Some-times we can't see the forest for the trees, or we think we are doing our job by getting all the work done. In fact, our job may go well beyond the separate pieces of work on our desks or even beyond making sure everyone else gets all their work done. Our jobs have more to do with staying connected to our long-term goals and vision. However, we can get caught up in the compulsiveness of doing everything. It can even become addictive. We believe we can escape the hard decisions of what to neglect if we can just work harder and longer and "get it all done."

> **"**
>
> *I really cannot give you the formula for success. But I can give you the formula for failure. It's this: Try to please everyone.*
>
> —Bernard Meltzer
> *Bernard Meltzer's Guidance for Living*
>
> **"**

ESCAPING THROUGH WORK

When we no longer can discern what things do *not* need to be done, we are in danger of slipping into dysfunctional work patterns. This dysfunction can range from burning the midnight oil too often to never having time for ourselves, our families, or our friends because everything seems to be important. When we lose our ability to distinguish the level of importance of tasks and find it easier to just stay at work and not have to deal with other parts of our lives, we have fallen into a full-blown case of workaholism.

Workaholism—Am I in Danger?

Awareness is the first step to recovery from workaholism. To see if you are falling into the trap, ask yourself these questions:

1 Does my personal identity and value as a person focus primarily on my job, career, job title, and professional or work expertise? Do I typically talk about my work, even at parties?

2 Do I challenge myself with accomplishing more than those around me and enjoy keeping a very full schedule, frequently working more than twelve hours a day?

3 Do I typically set unusually high work goals for myself and others, make extra-long to-do lists, and pride myself on being more productive than most people, focusing primarily on work?

4 Do I frequently bring work home, hoping to get a few steps ahead on my impossible work schedule by working after dinner, before bed, and in spurts all through the weekend?

5 Do I take a stack of work on vacation and find that I am frequently working while my family or friends are enjoying relaxation and recreational activities?

6 Do I frequently take work home that doesn't get looked at because I am just too exhausted to deal with it?

7 Do I find myself forgoing fun because I have brought work home and am afraid that if I get too involved in play, I won't get back to my work?

8 Do I find myself thinking wistfully of things I would like to enjoy but that take long periods of time, such as making a quilt, sailing, putting in a large garden, learning to play the piano, building model airplanes, learning golf or tennis, making wine, reading *War and Peace*, or going to the Olympics? Do I just think about them and not do them?

9 Do I feel anxious when I let a weekend go by without accomplishing anything?

10 Am I critical of my children, spouse, work colleagues, or friends who have a lot of fun in nonproductive activities? (They spend large blocks of time with "nothing to show for it.")

If you answered yes to many of these questions, you are probably tending toward workaholism and may be a candidate for burnout. Chapter Twelve has good ideas on ways you can turn this negative work profile around.

Workaholism has to do with losing ourselves in our work, blocking bad feelings, and numbing ourselves to pain or anxiety. When we fall into workaholism, we lose control of our lives and our time. We choose to feel like a victim of our work, our career, even our family. Aren't we working to support them? We feel trapped by our many responsibilities and believe we have no choice but to work longer and harder. *Choice* is the key word here. If we freely and joyfully choose to do what we are doing, because it has value and purpose for us, and we don't neglect our important relationships outside of work, that is not workaholism. But if we lose the option to choose and believe that we *have* to continue doing what we are doing, our work rules us. This is what workaholism is about.

Most symptoms of workaholism are also symptoms of a victim mentality, which is part of the workaholic profile. We feel that we no longer have a choice. We *have to* stay late or we might lose the bid. We *have* to take work home or the report won't be finished on time. We *have* to postpone our vacation or the audit won't get approved . . . and on and on. Each of these statements may be accurate in itself. But what would happen if we were prevented from doing this work because of circumstances out of our control?

"What If I Were to Fall Dead on the Spot?"

I was amazed, even shocked, when that very thing happened to someone I knew. When a key person dies, everyone shifts into a support mode and rallies around the family, meetings are held at work and a new organization is created, and frequently the new system is more efficient and productive than the old one was.

This frightened me at first, because I wanted to believe that I was indispensable and that the world would stop or be woefully lacking without my efforts. Without question, a person's talents and energy are missed and felt, but the point that came to me eventually is that there are always other ways to get things done and to accomplish goals. When I have gotten myself into a workaholic mind-set, part of the prison is my inability to see any alternative other than working harder and longer.

Frequently, long hours at work are a subconscious dodge for avoiding problems at home that seem unpleasant or overwhelming. If we have to be at work, how can we be faulted? We often avoid the responsibilities of parenthood or conflict with our mate by staying too busy to be available. It is less risky to be the partner who is off working and who only comes home in order to criticize the way the children are handled. This destructive behavior is an avoidance technique. Hiding behind fatigue and work demands, we feel entitled to be critical of our children or our mate.

"Is My Only Identity in My Work?"

Workaholism is also about having our primary, if not total, identity tied up in our work. We are valuable people if we succeed at work, and we are nobody if we are

less than the best. Money is the gauge of value whereas relationships have no hard currency. An alternative to workaholism is to choose a life of balance, with meaning invested in several directions. To find the time for this balance, we must learn how to let go. We need to find things that *don't* need doing.

USING EXECUTIVE NEGLECT

Ow do we determine what can be left undone? You will have to be the final judge, but here are some tips we have found helpful.

Reevaluate Routine Tasks

Purposely reevaluate routine business procedures or family chores to discover those that don't have to be done. What reports are no longer read or read by only a few people? What meetings are redundant, poorly led, or attended by everybody because no one has considered who is needed and who might be freed to accomplish other work?

When someone is ill or out with a family emergency, we create ways to get the job done with fewer people, even when we think we can't. In these situations, we are forced to let go of some tasks. After the fact, we find that we have discovered many ways of shifting gears and accomplish-

What Are Your Values?

The motivation for learning to let go of tasks is to have a firm idea of what you would gain from freeing up this extra time. The goal is not just to replace it with more work. If you haven't stopped recently to think about what is important to you, what your values are, and how you are going to achieve balance in your life, now would be a good time to do this. As you write out your personal values and mission, you might define your marriage or personal life, spiritual life, family, community interests, and hobbies as holding primary importance. Once you have this firmly planted in your mind, it will be easier to discover what tasks need your executive neglect.

A SPOTLESS HOUSE IS THE SIGN OF A MISSPENT LIFE!

ing more with less than could have happened without an emergency. However, the crisis was necessary to leverage us into the discovery of executive neglect. Isn't it interesting that this is almost impossible to do this without the drama of an emergency?

For example, one group of engineers came up with a very imaginative proposal for a client when they didn't have time to do the proposal in the standard way because a supervisor was stranded in a remote airport; instead, they had an intern draft a major section of the proposal. In another instance, a young couple discovered that they had made Christmas into an obligation with a trip home to visit both sets of parents every year. Last year, they all got the flu just before the holidays, and they discovered that they could enjoy Christmas much more without all the shopping, wrapping, decorating, and traveling. This year they are planning to stay home and enjoy a simplified Christmas at a less frantic pace.

In our business, we know we must make adjustments if team members are out sick or away for family emergencies. As a team, we have to laugh when we come dangerously close to burnout in the process of preparing for a major seminar on "How to Deal Effectively with Stress"! Together, we have learned to reevaluate options and create a reasonable workload by using existing materials rather than creating new ones, packing lighter for long-distance trips, or asking each person to pick up a part of the missing partner's responsibilities. Executive neglect can protect precious lives from needless burnout and expensive chronic illnesses— heart disease, hypertension, cancer, and ulcers are just a few of the most serious of the illnesses that can result from burnout. It doesn't take much imagination or judgment to just "get all the work done." Constant thought, imagination, and reevaluation of priorities are required to decide what does not need to be done and to save the time, energy, and sanity of co-workers.

Do not think that because you are "just an employee" or "just a secretary," you can't dare to use executive neglect. Let me encourage you to begin in your personal life. You may make an executive decision not to wash the car, not to do the laundry, or not to shop for groceries today. I find that when I am too busy to do some of these things, there is no great loss if they don't get done. Balancing responsibilities between your work, spouse, housework, and children provides a constant opportunity to use executive neglect. If choosing to spend time tossing a ball with your son and daughter means not mopping the kitchen floor this weekend, so be it. In the long term, a happy relationship is far more valuable than a clean floor.

Executive Neglect: GETTING STARTED

After looking over your to-do list for the week, flag at least two tasks for executive neglect. With practice, you may be able to flag even more. You are preplanning a few places to either "work skinny" or eliminate the task if the pressure from other projects becomes too great. Our team has found that by planning some options early in the week, we work with much more joy and accomplishment than if we assume the pressure of always having to do everything at the same standard of excellence.

Evaluate your results at the end of the week so that you can decide for yourself what the tradeoff is and how best to use this technique. You might discover that if you don't practice executive neglect and purposely choose what is less important at the beginning of the day or week, the fast speed of change will play havoc with your schedule and chance will squeeze out a few really important projects that you can't afford to neglect or drop.

Invest in Long-Term Solutions

I gathered two great ideas from creative parents. One busy mom invited her two sons, ages ten and fifteen, to start a catering business. She frequently entertained business and community

> 66
>
> *There is no pleasure in having nothing to do; the fun is in having lots to do and not doing it.*
>
> —Mary Little
>
> 99

leaders and needed their help. But to make it fun and challenging for them, she encouraged them to make it a business. Then she showed them how businesses get paid based on the quality of the food, service, and extra amenities they provide. By bringing

more imagination and initiative to their client (her), they could increase their fees. Her guests were genuinely impressed when the boys would prepare special dishes, select the perfect background music based on a guest's special interest, or provide excellent table service and then clean everything up while a pleasant business conversation began at the table.

"How do you manage this magic with your boys while the rest of the world struggles just to get teenagers to be civil?" a guest asked.

"It's called entrepreneurial spirit," she replied.

A second idea came from a father in El Paso, Texas. He invited his children to take turns writing checks and paying the family bills each month. He stayed involved in the process by signing the checks and was able to supervise the big picture.

But the unseen benefits were enormous. Not only did his two daughters, ages twelve and fifteen, get some practical experience in math and basic accounting, but they soon began to ask questions and make suggestions. For example, one mentioned at dinner how much the water bill had jumped that month and said that she had seen water running down the street when their sprinklers had been on too long. She also encouraged the family members to turn off the lights, television, and other appliances when they were not in use. It became a game for the family to team in lowering monthly expenses, and as a reward they celebrated or even took a special vacation on any money they saved over regular expenses.

This father saved several hours each month by delegating the routine part of paying bills, and in the process, his daughters became far more money-conscious, because they understood the big picture and felt valuable and part of the process.

Discuss Tasks You Choose to Neglect with Those Your Decision Affects

Talking about executive neglect and celebrating its application can help your team members learn from each other. No one person can make the best decisions every time. What I think can drop through the cracks without any repercussions, our bookkeeper may need and be depending on me to supply. Discussion and feedback will improve your judgment on which things you can purposely neglect.

Stopping the Cycle of Replies

Colleen Barrett, executive vice president for customers and corporate secretary at Southwest Airlines, is a wonderfully creative role model of using executive neglect to put an end to unnecessary paperwork on the sending end.

When she sends an article or piece of valuable information, she typically will add, "No reply necessary." Also, she will note, "Unless I hear otherwise from you, I will assume that this decision has your approval." Then both she and her team save the time and hassle of one more phone call.

She excels at providing warm, friendly service and partnering while cutting out all the extra steps that convention may have built in to the process.

Executive Neglect May Mean "a Lick and a Promise"

Executive neglect does not always mean not doing a job. In some cases, it can mean doing the job less than perfectly—with only a lick and a promise. If you decide to play ball, you give the kitchen floor a quick sweep before going outside. Rather than writing the full report or not writing any report, you write a quick memo to those who are interested. Or you call someone on the phone for a brief, clarifying conversation rather than holding a full-blown meeting.

CREATING GAMES TO CLARIFY PRIORITIES

Here is a technique I accidentally found that helps me to be both more convergent and more creative. I will think, "What if I suddenly became a widow? How would I handle this without my spouse?" "If Duane can't go on this trip, how can I make it work alone and not exhaust my-self in the process?" "If a tornado were approaching, what would I grab before I got out?" Suddenly the imaginary crisis provides a new perspective that allows me to let go of many of the things I thought I "had" to do. Put yourself in a similar emergency situation. What are the essentials you would take care of first?

Because by definition you have become an executive when you have responsibility for more than you can personally achieve, the implication is that you are a leader of others. We are all executives in one or more areas of our lives. We have responsibilities in a variety of arenas, and wishes and hopes in even more.

It is essential, then, that we stop attempting to accomplish every detail before us and learn to discern the important from the less important. Fun and humor will help speed this process as you create games for yourself out of your pile of responsibilities. In the next chapter we'll uncover some nasty—yet elusive—Time Bandits and provide you with strategies to reclaim precious quality time.

*Learning to let go
of past habits, outdated priorities,
and old perspectives
so that you can see everything
with fresh eyes
is essential
to making the best use
of your time.*

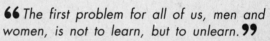

Time Bandits:
WHEN *inflexible*
RULES STEAL OUR
PRECIOUS TIME

17

> 66 The first problem for all of us, men and women, is not to learn, but to unlearn. 99
>
> —Gloria Steinem

> 66 Procrastination is the thief of time, unless it is really your intuition. Then it may be saving you from yourself. 99
>
> —Edward Young
> *Night Thoughts*

> 66 Don't put no constrictions on da people. Leave 'em ta hell alone. 99
>
> —Jimmy Durante

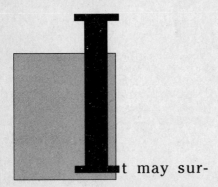

I
t may sur-
prise you to learn that the very
things that helped you to successfully
complete the journey through childhood may
be robbing you of time and energy today. But it is
nonetheless true that many of the rules you learned
and that helped you then are most likely counterproductive for you today. It is vitally important that you rewrite those indelible
rules to fit the many changes that
have taken place in your
life and responsibilities.

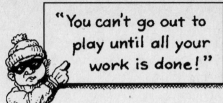

"You can't go out to play until all your work is done!"

Do you remember as a kid being told that you had to finish your work before you could go out to play? Did you learn that lesson so well that now it is difficult to play because your work never seems to be finished?

Think back to when you were a kid. How long did it take you to finish your work? Probably you had homework and some chores around the house. At that time in your life, you could finish your work in forty-five minutes to an hour. Then you were off to play ball, ride your bike, or enjoy other adventures with friends.

For the sake of contrast, close your eyes and imagine yourself in your workplace. Look around you and estimate how long it would take to complete everything waiting for your attention. You might pull out your desk drawers and glance over all the stuff that's waiting there "until you have some time." Rummage through the file cabinets. Isn't there some work that isn't urgent but is still waiting for you?

Now, still in your imagination, go home and look around to estimate how long it might take for you to get completely caught up with all your work there. Look in the garage, the closets, the attic. Think of your parents and extended family whom you have promised to visit or write to or take on a trip. What about the basketball hoop you promised to put up? Expand your thinking to include community activities. The fund-raising drive is coming up, and you said that you would chair it. Last year you promised to teach a Sunday School class—next year. What else is waiting for your time and attention?

When we were kids, other people had to point out what needed to be done. Our rooms could be a wreck, and we might not even notice. Certainly the trash could sit there for weeks without us ever feeling the urge to take it out. Even when someone else—our mother or father—made a list of chores, the list was relatively minimal.

That is no longer true. As adults with both imagination and a sense of responsibility, we find that the more we accomplish, the more there is to do. In other words, *there is no such thing as getting all of our work done!* From this perspective, it is evident that the rules we learned as children no longer apply. In most cases, they certainly need to be modi-

217

fied. The rule that said "You can't play until you get all your work done" might be changed to something like "Balancing hard work with carefree, childlike play is essential to good health," or "Enjoying refreshing play can be as important as accomplishing meaningful work," or even "Unless you take a break to enjoy refreshing play, you'll never get your work done!"

Once you have developed a keen sense of responsibility and the desire to serve and contribute to the world, effective work cannot continue for long without the balance of enjoyment.

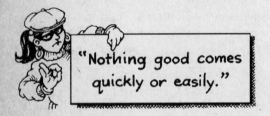

"Nothing good comes quickly or easily."

Most of the people I talk to suffer from the classic problem of overworking. We who rise to levels of higher responsibility in our jobs have to constantly fight our natural tendency to bring home stacks of work on a regular basis. Often we are so tired that all we can do is bring it home, where it sits in the corner and gathers guilt. That guilt is ready to jump on our shoulders the next morning when we pick up the stack of untouched papers to take back to the office. By the time we enter the office, we are already feeling worn out, discouraged, and generally crummy rather than refreshed and renewed.

The problem with this pattern is that short term it pays off big in rewards and recognition, but long term it becomes a trap. No award is big enough to satisfy our need to achieve. We no longer perform from an intrinsic desire to contribute, but from an extrinsic need to please others, break records, and be the best. This looks good on the surface, but it can take us into long-term burnout. And this condition is very contagious. When we are in burnout, our judgment is impaired. We go into denial, unable to admit when we are wrong and unable to hear warnings from others. When things go awry, we try to fix them the only way we know how to—we work harder and longer. Our example first inspires, then intimidates others into trying to match our hours and dedication.

This is a classic misuse of time. How much of this need to be the best describes you now or at some other time in your life? Do you have an early warning system to alert you when you are becoming a workaholic on this treadmill of delusion? Do you

218

then use your own personal process of balancing work with refreshing play to keep your judgment fresh and open and your health sound?

> "If you can't say something nice, don't say anything at all."

This is another rule we learned as children that may be blocking healthy communication and interactive teaming. Time is lost when we don't have the skills to express our views in healthy, open ways. When we store up bad feelings and anger because we don't have inner permission to voice our concerns and hold others accountable, we end up either resenting them because we get stepped on, overlooked, or abused, or storing up hurt and anger until one day it explodes in uncontrollable rage. Then, while we are out of control, we really might hurt others. In a situation

Am I in Balance?

The following list of questions is designed to help you assess the level of balance you have created in your life. If you can say yes to them, you are developing attitudes and habits that create balance in your life.

1 Do I typically look forward to my day at work? Am I eager to get up and get in to the job, and do I feel fulfilled at the end of most work days?

2 Do I have an equal enthusiasm for weekends and other days away from my job? Have I created an equally exciting and interesting life away from my job?

3 Do I have equal passion for a variety of interests other than work, such as golf, painting, backpacking, or gardening?

4 Do I have five or six close friends I spend time with at least six times a year who are not connected to my work?

5 Do I put a priority on quality time with my spouse and children, planning shared activities that we can all enjoy anticipating, doing, and then remembering?

6 Am I good at creating several brief moments of fun all through my day? Do I wear my professionalism lightly and encourage others to have fun along with me?

219

Without Play, We Can Fall into Traps

Even if we love our work and are energized by it, we can fall into some unhealthy traps.

1 *Our egos become fused with our work.* This results in a feeling of worthlessness if we are not constantly accomplishing. *We are not our work.* One of the dangers of this life-style is that we can become one-dimensional and have nothing to fall back on if we do lose our job or our business goes bankrupt. Having a balanced set of values and joys gives us each a safety net that can improve the quality of our investment, even in our work.

2 *We are so involved in our work that we take our marriage, our friendships, and our extended families for granted.* We miss out on the richness of experience that is sitting there waiting for us. (I look at my now-grown son and deeply regret the years of his childhood I missed out on. It is a precious part of my life I can never regain.) It's easy for us to overlook the day-to-day treasures such as nurturing our children and mates. Then one day, we wake up and it's too late.

3 *We are better at work than we are at interpersonal relationships, so we avoid them.* We may be highly rewarded for our work, but in fact, the more prestige we have, the more vulnerable we are to this trap. CEOs, entrepreneurs, brilliant engineers, and other high achievers may find themselves "too busy to deal with family issues," not realizing that down deep they don't like the anxiety of not knowing how to solve family problems and control family members the way they can control the people who work for them. So they conveniently stay too busy to deal with issues in areas where they are not succeeding. Losing a marriage or alienating a child is a high price to pay for living out of balance.

4 *Enjoying the euphoria of achieving difficult goals and winning big successes can be addictive.* We may then become single-focused and unwilling to expose ourselves to situations where we aren't the expert or in control. We don't take up new hobbies or we participate less and less if we are not excelling. Pretty soon all we are doing is our work. Our life becomes terribly out of balance without our even noticing.

5 *When we are around others who are not in our field, we have nothing to talk about and no way to share with them.* As a result, we see less and less of them and become more and more isolated in our specialty. If we do have opportunities to get out and enjoy totally different conversations, we may not know how to be curious and interested in topics beyond our experiences. This is an art to be cultivated and practiced. Today, with the world changing faster and faster, it is becoming increasingly important to learn and hear about views, interests, opinions, and perspectives that are different from our own.

like this, it is our hurt speaking, not a balanced person asking for accountability or insight. The unhealthy behavior pattern of never expressing our concerns can slow us down, hurt our team, and wreck our lives.

Learn to voice honest concerns and uncomfortable feelings early in ways that invite the other person's perspective or view on the subject. Learn to be curious and gather information instead of accusing, labeling, or blaming. A lot of time is lost when we lack the skills to keep communication open and to express our views in healthy, open ways. Sometimes we experience this "bite-your-tongue!" phenomenon when others derail our time management plans. Our priorities don't match, and someone has to give. Having been taught to "be nice," we hold it back, and those who are loudest usually prevail.

The situation might unfold like this: A member of our work team hands us a report and says, "I need this section of the report completed by one o'clock so we can add it to the final copy and make a FedEx deadline by 6:00 P.M." We are in the middle of another project that also has to be done immediately. We have a couple of choices. First, we can grit our teeth, bury our anger and frustration, and work double-fast

to get both things done. If we take this route, the quality of the work may suffer, but we won't have to confront anyone or risk anyone's displeasure. Or we can say immediately, "I'm sorry, George, I'm in the middle of the Robinson proposal. Let's talk about it a minute and see which one is more important to get done by five o'clock." In this case, we don't have to get mad at George at all, and together we can work out a win-win solution to the problem. It may not always happen as easily as that, but our goal is to keep the dialogue going until a solution is reached. If George says, "I don't care how you do it, but do them both!" we might explain that we can do this, but one or both of the projects will suffer in quality because of the need to rush through them. We might say, "Maybe you see a solution that I don't. Can you help me?" If we keep George talking and listening, our chances for a good solution will improve.

"Anything worth doing is worth doing well."

I wonder why children are taught this rule?

It's another major Time Bandit and a time trap as well. If you think it's wrong of me to challenge this statement, try getting curious instead.

I recall that as children, most of us really didn't have standards for our performance. If we wanted to do something such as learning to ride a bike with no hands or race around an obstacle course, we might really work at it. But if a task wasn't important to us, we might rush through it with very little awareness of excellence or even competence. (When I swept the kitchen each evening, my goal was to get outside and play, not to take pride in a clean kitchen floor completely free of crumbs.) We were usually given this rule in reference to something we didn't want to do in the first place. Our parents never invoked the rule when we were trying to reach the ceiling by jumping on the bed. Instead, they wanted us to establish some sense of accomplishment when we had completed tasks that were necessary, but not necessarily fun.

Over the years, achievers learn the lesson of taking pride in a job well done. But we can lose the ability to judge the relative importance of tasks. When is a job worth doing, but not worth our best effort? At first it may seem that the answer to this question should be "Never," but let me give you a way to test your response. At the beginning of a day, look over your list or schedule of what you plan to do and decide which projects on your list deserve your very best effort, which of them might do fine with an 80 percent effort, and which, if any, could get by on an effort of 50 percent or less. Many people start out in the morning blindly attempting to do everything perfectly. Toward late afternoon, some things either don't get done or get a tired effort at best (perhaps 50 to 70 percent), because that's all the time and energy that are left.

Alan Lakein tells us in his book, *How to Get Control of Your*

> **No executive I know ever looked back on his or her life and said, 'I wish I had spent more time at work.'**
>
> —A corporate leader

222

Time and Your Life, "The 80/20 rule says, 'If all items are arranged in order of value, 80 percent of the value would come from only 20 percent of the items, while the remaining 20 percent of the value would come from 80 percent of the items.'" We should learn to save our best efforts for that significant 20 percent of the projects on our to-do lists. We still have to sweep the kitchen floor, but now, depending on our energy and schedule, we can decide how much effort to put into it. Sometimes a quick whisk is sufficient. At other times, it must be done thoroughly, and we can decide when that time is.

Would you rather let fate or happenstance decide which projects get your 100 percent effort, or would you like a say in the matter? If you would like to decide, I encourage you to begin choosing in advance a task to do quickly at 50 percent effort to free you to accomplish other, more significant, tasks at 90 to 100 percent. Then celebrate your courage. Evaluate your results so you can learn as you go.

When I am preparing for an important business presentation, I can go to the hairdresser, get a fresh manicure, and spend the usual forty-five minutes packing for my trip. Or I can shampoo in the shower, do a touch-up on my

> *If you only do things you can do perfectly, you stop learning new skills, stop taking chances, and stop having fun.*

nails, and pack in twenty minutes so that I can spend the extra time preparing for my speech and enjoying quality time with my husband. Over the years, having the courage to commit to 60 percent grooming so that I can stay 90 or 100 percent in love with my husband has been a good tradeoff.

You have to decide for yourself. I know that to attempt to be perfect is to limit yourself. If you only do things you can do perfectly, you stop learning new skills, stop taking chances, and stop having fun. I get far more excellence out of my work and my personal life now that I am starting to learn to put my effort where it counts and not worry about the small stuff.

18

Let's Celebrate!
YOU'VE EARNED YOUR PH.D. IN **TIME MANAGEMENT!**

66 When we can begin to take our failures nonseriously, it means we are ceasing to be afraid of them. It is of immense importance to laugh at ourselves. 99

—Katherine Mansfield

66 Cherish forever what makes you unique, 'cuz you're really a yawn if it goes! 99

—Bette Midler

225

I hope I have challenged you with many new ways to think about, use, and enjoy time. This book has shared with you some biases our society has toward people who think and manage time in different ways. With the time management system you will design for yourself, along with your new time management skills, you will be better equipped to deal with the challenges ahead.

How can we know that we have a balanced, whole-brained way of living our lives and investing our precious time? Here are seven measures our team has found extremely useful:

226

1. We enjoy both organizing *and* using our system. This means that we have designed a system that fits our unique needs and has open-ended flexibility; it's designed for the fast changes and unexpected events that are becoming part of the norm in our culture.

2. We intuitively know when our system is no longer working for us and others; we continue to create options until our new system is again balanced and working effectively.

3. We look forward to and enjoy both work *and* frequent joy breaks. Trust and thoughtfulness are used to plan joy breaks, rather than allowing them to be splurges or binges. At first, when we are mostly out of balance, we may find it hard to get ourselves back to work if we spend time outside in the sun. Or we may find that we spend too much money if we allow ourselves to buy toys or other fun stuff, just for the enjoyment they bring us. We may eat too much when we stop for a joy break that includes cake or cookies. We must be gentle with ourselves and keep experimenting with ways to bring about a satisfying balance. Often, when our little-kid self first takes control, it is so glad to be out and has such low trust for our adult part that it says, "Make hay while the sun shines! I don't get to have fun often, so I'm going to milk this for all it's worth!" We know we are in balance when our adult self and our little-kid self listen to each other, trust each other, and mutually cooperate.

4. As we learn to balance the needs of our right-brained child and our left-brained adult, we begin to experience less internal conflict and more peace, centeredness, and joy. We know when we need to work and when we need to play. We know when we need to spend money for pleasure and when we need to save money and stick to a budget. We know when we need to eat sensibly for energy and when we need to have a hot fudge sundae.

5. We care just as much about how our time management system affects others as how it works for us. We enjoy the support, partnering, and appreciation of those around us because our system honors the differences of the significant others in our lives. In other words, we don't say, "I need a system that works for

Throw a "No PDS" Party

On one occasion, we were working late to meet a deadline, and everyone on our team was pretty spent. So we threw a five-minute "No PDS" party. We put on some lively music and rounded up some soft drinks, juice, and cookies; then we celebrated getting this far with "No Prisoners Taken, No Deaths, and No Suicides!"

This bit of nonsense lightened up a tense, tiring situation and helped everyone relax for a few minutes so we could renew ourselves enough to finish up and go home in a better frame of mind. Sometimes when you feel under the pressure of time and work, it pays to celebrate!

me. To heck with everybody else. It's their problem if they can't deal with my structure or unpredictability. That's just me." Instead, we satisfy our needs as well as those of our opposites.

6. On most days, we can transform the negative things that happen to us into challenge and opportunity, with surprisingly positive outcomes.

7. We feel that we genuinely get to enjoy both work and play.

IT'S TIME TO CELEBRATE!

It may surprise you to learn that celebrations are a great way to expand your time management style. Every time you explore, share, practice, or master a new skill or concept, celebrate! Become an expert at celebrations—two-minute celebrations, day-end celebrations, early-morning celebrations, end-of-the-week celebrations, "lessons learned" celebrations, "we did it" celebrations, and monthly, quarterly, and annual celebrations. Make them frequent, make them spontaneous, and make them fun.

Anne Albright, executive vice president of Wyndham Incentive Marketing in Dallas, says:

"It is important to stop and notice what has been accomplished, in addition to how much remains to be done. It was only a few months ago that I realized that I was always focused on unfinished work, on the projects ahead of me. When a finished project came in, no one in the office even paused for a breath! We were all under the gun of the next deadline. Now, I run around and at least get everyone to admire the new 'Share the Air' marketing piece and have a moment of celebration."

Jeanne Patterson, purchasing and distribution manager of Express Services in Oklahoma City, makes creative rewards a part of celebrations:

"We often have drawings to see who can go home early, have a half-day off, or come in late. Little unexpected surprises make employees feel special."

Will celebrations really make a significant difference in your time management style? Go back to what you know about thinking styles. Discipline, routine, sticking to a plan, and practice are

> # *There's no reason that work has to be suffused with seriousness. . . . Professionalism can be worn lightly. Fun is a stimulant to people. They enjoy their work more and work more productively.*
>
> —Herb Kelleher, CEO, Southwest Airlines Company

229

primarily left-brained processes, while celebrations represent the right-brained style. If you blend the two daily, with one supporting and complementing the other, you gain a tremendous momentum—much like a cycler taking a big hill. Pumping with both legs gives you a speed that you could never achieve by pedaling on only one side of the bike with only one leg.

The work-play, practice-celebrate, experiment-apply, risk-evaluate cycle moves you back and forth between brain hemispheres, drawing on the varied talents and motivation of both the left and right brain. Weaving the parts of your brain into interdependent partners and using teamwork through balancing activities brings you a tremendous synergy.

Try it with yourself and your friends, family, and work partners. Combined with the other techniques in this book, it will help you to find hours you never knew you had. It will also help you to enjoy the hours you spend—at work, at play, away from home, or at home—with your family, friends, and co-workers. That is the true goal of time management—giving you the time you want to do all you want to do, and allowing you to do it joyfully. We've found that these techniques have worked for us and for others. We hope they have worked just as well for you.

It's time for you to celebrate!

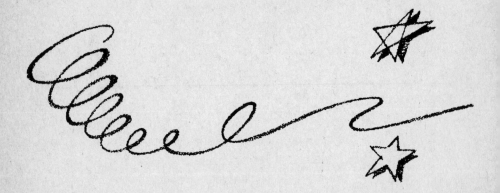

230

Final Thoughts...

TIME-LIFE MANAGEMENT:
From a Linear Discipline to a Holistic Dance

> **"**I can live out of my imagination instead of my memory.**"**
>
> —Stephen Covey
> *The Seven Habits of Highly Effective People*

> **"**All people dream; but not equally. Those who dream by night in the dusty recesses of their minds wake in the day to find that it was vanity. But the dreamers of the day are the dangerous people, for they may act their dream with open eyes to make it possible.**"**
>
> —T. E. Lawrence

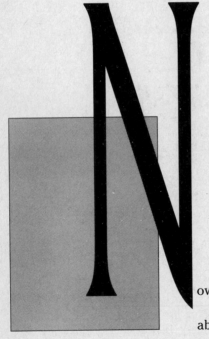

ow that you have thought a lot about the big picture of time management and the reality of time, here are some final thoughts.

IS IT THE BEST OF TIMES OR THE WORST OF TIMES?

A few decades ago, technology was touted as the way to give people endless free time. Machines would do our work and our new challenge would be to figure out how to use this leisure time. If we wished, we could sit back and eat bonbons. As it has evolved, however, technology has saved time on individual tasks, but by doing this, it has also made us go faster to keep up. From fax machines to mobile cellular telephones, from E-mail to tablet-sized computers with eight megabytes of memory, from instantaneous news from around the globe to interactive television, technology has served both to speed up the rate at which business and communication happen and to increase manyfold the amount of information we expect to absorb, understand, and put to use. We are told that before the turn of the century, we will all have available to us five times the amount of data that we deal with now.

Currently, information doubles every twenty-plus months, and already it is a big challenge to keep pace. How will we cope with five times that amount? Technology is obviously part of the answer. Computers can easily deal with large amounts of data. Those who are still computer-illiterate are already behind. Becoming a student and participant in the constantly changing world of technology is essential. Nevertheless, technology is not the whole answer.

Technology in itself tends to make us want to go faster and faster, because the machines go faster and faster. I fax you a letter; you fax me back. A communication that ten years ago would have taken at least a week can be completed in a couple of hours. Technology also demands that we spend time learning how to operate these new machines. But as soon as we know a program, it becomes obsolete, or is upgraded, or is replaced by one that is even better, and we are challenged to relearn, unlearn, or learn more. Thus we feel even more time pressure from ever-changing technological developments. Not only are we challenged to invest time in learning new technologies; we also have to let go of old habits and beliefs about the way things should be done. That is often an emotional as well as a time drain.

As we try to go faster and faster, we are also learning from science and holistic medicine about new illnesses. Hurry sick-

ness is directly tied to a sense of time speeding by, to the feeling that one has to rush to beat the clock, to the belief that faster is better. As more and more work piles up and we hurry to complete it, we find that our health declines. The Japanese are concerned with a trend where people in business literally work themselves to death and even give it a special name. In this country we have known for years that Type-A personalities, who work all the time, rarely enjoy recreation, and feel compulsive about getting everything done, are prime candidates for early death and disability.

We are at a unique point in history when everything seems to have speeded up. Alvin Toffler, in *The Third Wave*, discussed how in the history of the world we moved from a nomadic society into the agrarian age, then into the industrial age, and now into the information age. But the third wave, into the information age, was just the beginning. In the past two decades, a series of tsunami-sized waves has shaken our perception of time—the age of microchip computer technology, the age of neuroscience, and the post–Cold War age of shifting from a local to a global society. We have found that we are using only a fraction of our brainpower. Dealing with other cultures, which may be changing as quickly as we are, affects our perception of time and how we behave in business and social exchanges. We must learn more, adjust more, accept more change, and rethink more than ever before.

IT IS WHAT WE MAKE IT!

Suddenly we find that we are participating in simultaneous waves of change that allow us not only to experience many different perceptions of time, but to become ever more aware of the power of our beliefs over our destiny. We have choices at every turn. We can imagine ourselves victims of new technology and become beaten down (or overwhelmed). Or we can find creative ways to use new tech-

nology as an extension of our own brains. We can decide whether or not to send the fax. We can store information in the computer and draw from it only when we need it. And as we sense the pressures building to move faster, work harder, and accomplish more, we can choose to take charge of our environment.

One way is by building teams that offer support with a rich variety of gifts and strengths. Another is by consciously choosing to play, to laugh, and to indulge the child within in order to refresh, renew, and rejuvenate ourselves. If we feel stressed and overloaded, we can stop the cycle of denial and guilt and instead pause to look at our life goals and recognize that each moment is a piece of a complex tapestry we are weaving to please ourselves and those we care about. We can change the design, insert new threads, and even applaud the parts that are imperfect. We develop an innate knowledge that tells us when our habits are obsolete, our bodies are weary, and our brains are tired.

We can learn from other cultures—taking the best knowledge and thought in the world—and create a new understanding of time. No longer are we tied to a simplistic, linear perspective. If it is true that time is something invented in our minds by our belief systems, then it is possible to create still another totally different sense of time. Albert Einstein taught us that time is relative. Two of his statements provide stimulating insights:

"Imagination is more important than knowledge. For while knowledge defines all we currently know and understand, imagination points to all we might yet discover and create."

"I simply imagine it so, then go about to prove it."

As we study how the brain and mind work, we realize that the process of holding a dream or a vision clearly in mind is the first step toward finding the path from current reality to this new reality. We now know that neuro-chemically, when we hold an exciting or inspiring dream clearly in mind, the chemical makeup in our brain changes, which actually transforms the way we think. Einstein may have been intuitively way ahead in realizing that imaging takes us halfway to a solution. In order to explore creatively, we must overcome our scripting that says, "Daydreaming is a waste of time."

There is now a tremendous amount of interest in and focus on the stages of growth in mental health. In this field, we are becoming aware that a child's perception of time is very different from an adult's. More and more, little by little, we are realizing that clocks don't keep track of time as much as our own perception of time creates the reality that can then either enslave us or free us to savor each moment. We can use our intuition to create whole new options, giving us all the time, resources, and possibilities we could ever need. Otherwise, we may find ourselves rushing to complete our step in an assembly line, too busy to notice that the product of our efforts has become obsolete.

Choosing to be a designer, engineer, and cocreator of our concept of time rather than a reactive, helpless passenger waiting for fate to deal the cards can make a great difference in the quality of our lives. It allows us to grasp the unlimited possibilities that exist and to create a life of quality, meaning, purpose, and joy by becoming our unique selves and unfolding the genius of our individual gifts. We realize that our brains are more than data banks of old information; instead, they are infinitely expandable and mysterious resources that can create the new reality of our future.

By learning to become more whole-brained, we can all expand our horizons, stay balanced, contribute unmatched excellence, and enjoy every moment of life. Exciting new insights, skills, and concepts are just waiting to be incorporated into our understanding of life and time. It's too late to merely get organized in order to manage time. Today we need a whole-brained solution that includes teaming, understanding the way our brains work, sharpening our communication skills, and shifting from a black-and-white world to one filled with brilliant, but often contradictory, colors. We can learn to live with and celebrate paradox—and in paradox and paradigm shifts we find a deeper understanding of time and time management.

Finally, time management becomes a way to design our present moment and our future, to shift from a discipline into an art that includes our ethics, our spirituality, and who we understand ourselves to be. The choice is there for each of us.

AFTERWORD
by Duane Trammell

In 1982, my friend and mentor, Dr. Ann McGee-Cooper, invited me to join her in a project on rethinking time management. Working with a team of gifted and talented students and their teachers, we designed a book for teachers and students based on right- and left-brain thinking styles. We wanted to experiment with more enjoyable ways of organizing, keeping lists and calendars, and accomplishing work. Added to our system would be a healthy dose of play—an element that was especially important to me because Ann had helped me to rediscover it.

Many of the ideas in this book were born in our first version, published in 1983. In addition to students and teachers, businesses and organizations were fascinated with the ideas and added to our understanding of the concepts. It amazes me to think about how much the world has changed since we published the first version. In 1982, our newly purchased personal computer was top-of-the-line. It filled a huge desktop, and the daisy wheel proudly sputtered out chapters in fifteen-minute increments. At that time, it seemed instantaneous.

Now, our laser printer quietly purrs and prints the same amount in less than two minutes.

For the first book, we drove over to the publisher's office for weekly meetings and laid out all of the pages to discuss. These meetings usually took more than half a day. As we finished up the last draft of this book, Ann was in one city, the publisher was in another, the book designer was at another location, the illustrator was working from his home, and I was in Dallas editing. We communicated hourly by phone, fax, and overnight delivery—just as if we were all in the same room.

Although new technology speeds up our processes and saves us time, we have yet to find all this "extra" time. There will always be important things pressuring us to hurry faster, to work harder, and to accomplish more. Working on this manuscript with Ann has reminded me once again that *we* are the only ones who can slow ourselves down to reclaim a deeply satisfying balance within our lives. It's a lesson that we relearn daily.

Bibliography

Albrecht, Karl. *Brain Power*. Englewood Cliffs, N.J.: Prentice-Hall, 1980.

Allenbaugh, Eric. *Wake-Up Calls*. Austin, Tex.: Discovery Publications, 1992.

Armstrong, David M. *Managing by Storying Around: A New Method of Leadership*. New York: Doubleday, 1992.

Begley, Sharon, Wright, Lynda, Church, Vernon, and Hager, Mary. "Mapping the Brain." *Newsweek,* April 20, 1992, pp. 66–70.

Bogen, Joseph E., and Gazzaniga, Michael. "Cerebral Commissurotomy in Man: Minor Hemisphere Dominance for Certain Visuospatial Functions." *Journal of Neurosurgery,* July–December 1965, *23.*

Bogen, Joseph E., and Vogel, Phillip J. "Cerebral Commissurotomy in Man—Preliminary Case Report." *Bulletin of the Los Angeles Neurological Society,* 1962, *27,* 169–172.

Buzan, Tony. *Use Both Sides of Your Brain*. New York: Dutton, 1974.

Csikszentmihalyi, Mihaly. *Flow: The Psychology of Optimal Experience*. New York: HarperCollins, 1990.

Cooper, M., and Aygen, M. "Effect of Medication on Blood Cholesterol and Blood Pressure." *Journal of the Israel Medical Association,* 1978, *95*(1).

Copeland, Lennie, and Griggs, Lewis. *Going International*. New York: Plume, 1986.

Covey, Stephen R. *The 7 Habits of Highly Effective People*. New York: Simon & Schuster, 1989.

Dossey, Larry. *Beyond Illness: Discovering the Experience of Health*. Boston: New Science Library, 1984a.

Dossey, Larry. *Healing Words*. New York: HarperCollins, 1993.

Dossey, Larry. *Space, Time & Medicine*. Boston: New Science Library, 1984b.

Dossey, Larry. *Recovering the Soul*. New York: Bantam Books, 1989.

Dossey, Larry. *Meaning & Medicine*. New York: Bantam Books, 1991.

Ferguson, Marilyn. *The Aquarian Conspiracy*. Los Angeles: J. P. Tarcher, 1980.

Fisher, Roger, and Ury, William. *Getting to Yes.* New York: Penguin Books, 1981.

Friedman, Meyer, and Rosenman, Ray H. *Type A Behavior and Your Heart.* New York: Knopf, 1974.

Getzels, J. W., and Jackson, P. W. *Creativity and Intelligence: Explorations with Gifted Students.* New York: Wiley, 1962.

Greenleaf, Robert K. *The Servant as Leader.* Newton Centre, Mass.: Robert K. Greenleaf Center, 1970.

Gross, Scott. *Positively Outrageous Service.* New York: MasterMedia Ltd., 1991.

Guildford, J. P. *Creativity and Its Cultivation.* New York: HarperCollins, 1959.

Hall, Edward T. *Beyond Culture.* New York: Anchor Books, Doubleday, 1976.

Hall, Edward T., and Hall, Mildred R. *Hidden Differences—Doing Business with the Japanese.* New York: Anchor Books, Doubleday, 1987.

Hall, Edward T., and Hall, Mildred R. *Understanding Cultural Differences.* Yarmouth, Maine: Intercultural Press, 1990.

Hanson, Gayle. "Japan at Play." *Insight on the News,* April 27, 1992, *8*(17), 6–37.

Harper, Bob, and Harper, Ann. *Skill-Building for Self-Directed Team Members.* New York: MW Corporation, 1992.

Herrmann, Ned. *Herrmann Brain Dominance Instrument.* Lake Lure, N.C.: The Ned Herrmann Group, Applied Creative Services, Ltd., 1989, 1990, 1991. For information call (704) 625-9153, fax (704) 625-2198.

Human Synergistics Inc. *SCOPE Leader's Guide.* Plymouth, Mich.: Human Synergistics Inc., 1984.

Imai, Masaaki. *Kaizen: The Key to Japan's Competitive Success.* New York: Random House, 1986.

Lakein, Alan. *How to Get Control of Your Time and Your Life.* New York: New American Library, 1973.

Lewis, David, and Greene, James. *Thinking Better.* New York: Rawson-Wade, 1982.

McGee-Cooper, Ann. *You Don't Have to Go Home from Work Exhausted!* Dallas: Bowen & Rogers, 1990; New York: Bantam, 1992.

McGinnis, Alan Loy. *The Power of Optimism.* San Francisco: HarperCollins, 1990.

McWilliams, John-Roger, and McWilliams, Peter. *Do It! Let's Get Off Our Buts.* Los Angeles: Prelude Press, 1991.

Marschall, Richard. *America's Great Comic Strip Artists.* New York: Abbeville Press, 1989.

Michalko, Michael. *Thinkertoys.* Berkeley, Calif.: Ten Speed Press, 1991.

Ornstein, Robert Evan. *The Psychology of Consciousness.* Longmont, Colo.: Viking Productions, 1972.

Peters, Tom. *Liberation Management.* New York: Knopf, 1992.

Restak, Richard M. *The Brain.* New York: Bantam, 1984.

Robbins, John. *Diet for a New America.* Walpole, N.H.: Stillpoint Publishing, 1987.

Scott, Dru. *How to Put More Time in Your Life.* New York: Dutton, 1984.

Segalowitz, Sid J. *Two Sides of the Brain.* Englewood Cliffs, N.J.: Prentice-Hall, 1983.

Senge, Peter M. *The Fifth Discipline.* New York: Doubleday, 1990.

Silverstein, Shel. *Where the Sidewalk Ends.* New York: HarperCollins, 1974.

Sperry, R. W. "The Great Cerebral Commissure." *Scientific American,* January 1964, *210*(1), 42–63.

Sperry, R. W. "Lateral Specialization in the Surgically Separated Hemispheres." In *The Neurosciences Third Study Program,* ed. F. O. Schmitt and F. G. Worden (pp. 1–19). Cambridge, Mass.: MIT Press, 1974.

Springer, Sally, and Deutsch, Georg. *Left Brain, Right Brain.* New York: W. H. Freeman, 1989.

Steinem, Gloria. *Revolution from Within.* Boston: Little, Brown, 1992.

Toffler, Alvin. *The Third Wave.* New York: Bantam, 1981.

Wagner, Jane. *The Search for Signs of Intelligent Life in the Universe.* New York: HarperCollins, 1987.

Wheatley, Margaret J. *Leadership and the New Science.* San Francisco: Berrett-Koehler, 1992.

Index

Play: and celebrations, 158–160, 228–230; childlike versus adult types of, 155–158; choice of, 235; and compounding time, 180, 185; exercises for, 150; guilt over, 170–171; importance of, 83, 146–148, 159–161, 217–218; and joy breaks, 73, 96–97, 123, 137, 152, 154, 167–169; and kid spirit, 18–19, 21, 137, 169–170; lack of, and denial, 147, 151; making time for, 158–159, 194; as not fun, 155–158; positive balance of work and, 151–152; and prioritizing, 212; and same-o, same-o disease, 148–149; scheduling of, 128–129; self-assessment on, 153. *See also* Kid spirit

Polychronic time: appropriate designation of, 37; in business, 26, 27, 33–36; characteristics of polychronic people, 28; and cultural differences, 27–32; definition of, 21, 25–26, 29; in home life, 32, 36–37; and mothers, ix, 32, 36–37; rationale for, 1; and time management, 83; tips for monochronic situations with polychronic needs, 35; tips for polychronic situations with monochronic expectations, 34; uses of, 25–27, 37

Positive self-talk, 97–99

Positron emission tomography (PET), 56

Post-it Notes, 93–94, 98, 118–119

Practicality versus science, 57

Prioritizing: allowing some tasks to die a natural death, 110; combining tasks to shorten list, 108; and feedback, 107–108; games for, 212; looking at individual tasks in context of big picture, 104–105; and outsourcing, 106–107; "quick and dirty" approach to, 109–110; and rethinking process, 107; and scheduling, 110–112; and thinking styles, 102–103; and too much to do and not enough time, 105–108; and trust, 106

Procrastination, 137, 139, 140

Productivity, drops in, 170

Progressive relaxation, 18

Proposals, drafting of, 109–110

"Quick and dirty" approach, 109–110

Recreation, 83. *See also* Play

Relaxation, 18

Reveal, T., 11

Rewards: for following the plan, 138; and planning, 93–99

Rhoades, A., 106–107

Right brain, left brain, 54–56, 70, 72, 83–84, 87

Role playing of saying no, 190

Rosenman, R. H., 16

Routine tasks, 207–209

Rush, B., 124

Rushing. *See* Hurry sickness

Ryerson Coil Processing, 135

Same-o, same-o disease, 148–149

Sarton, M., 145

Saying maybe, 197

Saying no: and blocking out entire commitment on calendar, 194–195; difficulty of, 188–190; gracious and firm ways of, 196–197; and networking, 196; role playing of, 190; and second opinion, 195–196; and self-esteem, 190–191; stigma of, in business, 191–192; strategies for, 193–197; and third right answer, 198

Saying yes, 192–193, 199

Scandinavia, 29

Scheduling: of clear, uninterrupted time, 123–124; color used in, 118–120, 123; and compounding time, 179–185; design of system for, 116–120; for energy, 121–123; of fragments of time, 123; and invisible time, 120–121; late-night work, 139–140; and making calendar visual and fun, 117–118; of overlooked pockets of time, 124; of play, 128–129; and polychronic time, 27; Post-it Notes used in, 118–119; and prioritizing, 110–112; and saying no, 194–195; team scheduling, 124–127; and traveling, 183–184; and types of calendars, 117

Schopenhauer, A., 8

Schweitzer, A., 179

Science, versus practicality, 57

Scott, D., 70

Secretaries, working with, 126–127

Self-assessment: on balance, 219; on contaminated time, 166; on fun, 153; on thinking styles and time management skills, 59–65; on workaholism, 204, 220

Self-esteem, 190–191

Self-talk, positive, 97–99

Slowing down, 17–21

Socrates, 24

Southwest Airlines, 21, 106–107, 179, 183–185, 211

Space, Time & Medicine (Dossey), 12

Spearman, D., 183

Sperry, R., 55

Spouses. *See* Home life

Springer, S., 54–55

SQUID (superconducting quantum interference device), 56

Standardization, 8

Steinem, G., 215

Stickers, on calendars, 119, 120

Stress, 147–148

Sugar, 160

Superconducting quantum interference device (SQUID), 56

Acknowledgments

Duane and I wish to thank all those special people whose patience, encouragement, and partnering have expanded our lives and made this book possible:

Ray Bard and his team:

Suzanne Pustejovsky
art director/designer/production coordinator

Helen Hyams
copyeditor

Mike Krone
illustrator

Michael Donahue
marketing consultant

Judy Barrett
writer

Jenny Edwards, who came to intern with us and collected scores of interviews and case studies for our research.

Dave Wilson, national director of professional development, Ernst & Young, who wrote a business draft of the manuscript in 1987 and encouraged us to continue toward this version with his editorial wit and wisdom.

Don and Judy Lambert and all of our many other readers. Judy, an inspiring author and teacher of writing, encouraged us over some rough spots.

Dr. Luis Martin, emeritus professor of history, Southern Methodist University, and director of the Intellectual Fitness Center, Perot Systems Corporation, who coached us on historical information.

The Unit 2 project management team at Comanche Peak, an interdependent team composed of leaders from six companies—Brown & Root, Inc., Bechtel Energy Corporation, Stone & Webster, Inc., ABB Impell, Inc., Westinghouse Electric Corporation, and Texas Utilities Company—five of which were considered competitors prior to this project. We give them credit for their whole-brained application of the concepts in this book and for creative and effective role modeling in a demanding, high-performance situation. They combined the highest possible standards of safety, quality, and continuous improvement of performance to reach new levels in the engineering and construction industry.

And finally, we thank our Dallas partners at Ann McGee-Cooper and Associates, Inc., present and past, and their families for sharing and living the vision of this book:

Carolyn Benard
Joyce Bennett
Tim Chamberlain
Linda Conger
Diane Cory
Jonnie Haug
Marybeth Hoesterey
Anna Irving
Janet Kirby
Rayo McCollough
Mike Mann
Jackie Maxwell
Karol Omlor
Kay Russell
Billie Snider
Georgia Ulrich
Stevie Womack

Together they have made it fun to do the impossible in less than ten minutes.

The Authors

Ann McGee-Cooper, Ed.D., is an author, lecturer, business consultant, creativity expert, and principal of Ann McGee-Cooper and Associates, Inc., of Dallas, Texas. But Ann is much more than a combination of titles. She has put her understanding of the mind's potential to work for major corporations and organizations such as The Prudential, Ernst & Young, Kodak, Texas Utilities, The Conference Board, MCI Business Markets, the Central Intelligence Agency, the American Heart Association, Fluor Daniel, Inc., Brown & Root, Inc., and many others. The message she shares with groups everywhere is one of hope: by valuing people and appreciating their differences, she shows that growth of abilities and talents is unlimited. She has also communicated this message through the publication, with her partner, Duane Trammell, of this book and of their first book, *You Don't Have to Go Home from Work Exhausted!* which offered creative strategies to help people find new reservoirs of energy by rediscovering their passion for fun, work, and life.

After earning degrees from the University of Texas at Austin and Southern Methodist University, Ann went on to design her own doctoral program at Columbia University focused on creative problem solving and the politics of change. She served on the faculty at Purdue University and taught creative thinking skills to science and engineering postdoctoral students preparing to work for NASA and other futuristic programs. She was assigned the task of awakening their latent creativity. Ann was, indeed, a pioneer, for at this time it was generally believed that creativity could not be taught. Ann demonstrated that it could.

Although she is highly gifted, these accomplishments did not come easily for Ann. While working with teachers at the Dean Learning Center in Dallas, she realized why most learning had been a struggle for her: she discovered that she exhibited many of the traits of dyslexia, hyperactivity, and attention deficit disorder.

Ann McGee-Cooper's journey with time management began when she was in the third grade. She recalls, "I have vivid memories of the panicked feeling I experienced when I was asked by the teacher to go out, look at the hall clock, and tell her the time. I must have been absent the day everyone else learned how to do this. Fortunately, an older student went by and I asked her the time. Filled with shame, I couldn't even bring myself to ask my family to teach me."

Thirty years later, she learned that she was profoundly dyslexic. Clocks still remained a puzzle. But along the way, she had created a new way to make sense out of time management. Ann relates, "All of the structure and rules that were offered as *the* solutions to time management problems only took me backward in frustration. Someone needed to create a new system that helped rather than hindered the divergent person."

The good news is that what Ann created has not only freed her to be far more productive and joyful each day; it has also opened the door for hundreds of other divergent visual processors. The old rules that tend to hold many people back have been broken and rewritten to create a new open-ended process that brings a whole-brained balance to life's growing demands and pleasures.

■ ■ ■ ■ ■

Duane Trammell is managing partner of Ann McGee-Cooper and Associates. A native of Dallas, Duane was educated in the public schools, where he began a love affair with teaching that has shaped his career and touched the lives of countless others. Duane chose to work in low-socioeconomic areas and to help develop a program for underachieving students with academic potential, but he found that the long hours and extra miles began to catch up with him. A workshop on burnout and the superhuman syndrome caught his eye, and there, in 1978, he met Ann McGee-Cooper.

Duane recalls, "Ann put me on the road back to recovery. In that workshop, she taught us how to create new options for guiltless play. It changed my life and the quality of my teaching." Indeed, it did. In the next five years, Duane was awarded the Dallas Teacher of the Year award, an award as One of the Outstanding Teachers in Texas, and the Ross Perot Award for Excellence in Teaching.

The business relationship between Ann and Duane started in 1981, when Ann asked Duane to teach with her at the University of Texas at Dallas. She then invited him to join her at Ann McGee-Cooper and Associates. Together, they wrote the first edition of *Time Management for Unmanageable People,* targeted for teachers and gifted students. They next collaborated on *You Don't Have to Go Home from Work Exhausted!* published in 1990.

When asked what he feels is most important about the time management philosophies he and Ann represent, Duane responds, "In working with scores of people, we have found that time management needed to be expanded to allow for two distinctly different ways of managing time. By recognizing these differences, we can all be more productive at accomplishing and, equally as important, we will have time for the things we most enjoy."

251

Share These Unique Time Management Strategies with Your Company or Group!

Ann McGee-Cooper and Duane Trammell are as opposite as night and day, yet they have developed a great partnership that calls upon the strengths of each of their styles. What better way for you to share these time management ideas with others at work than to see these strategies in action?

Fun is the key word here. Whether it's a keynote speech to open a conference, a half-day workshop offering to put some pizzazz back into a training program, or a ten-month development program to transform an organizational culture, Ann and Duane know how to make a learning experience fun and memorable. At any given moment, you may see a tap dance, watch cartoon characters magically appear on a flip chart, or be entertained by a tableful of mind-bending toys. And the best part is that you'll learn a dozen or more practical tips to improve both the productivity and quality of your life.

Time Management is only one of several programs available from Ann McGee-Cooper and Associates, Inc. Other areas of expertise include creativity, creative problem solving, interdependent teaming, personal energy management, and future skills. Special programs can be uniquely designed to fit your group. Recently Ann McGee-Cooper and Associates, Inc. has created programs for groups such as American Airlines, the CIA, the American Heart Association, the Federal Reserve Bank, Mary Kay Cosmetics, The Prudential, and Brown & Root, Inc.

Join the thousands who have participated with these award-winning coaches in a learning experience that will pay off with dividends in performance and attitude by calling

Ann McGee-Cooper and Associates
214-357-8550

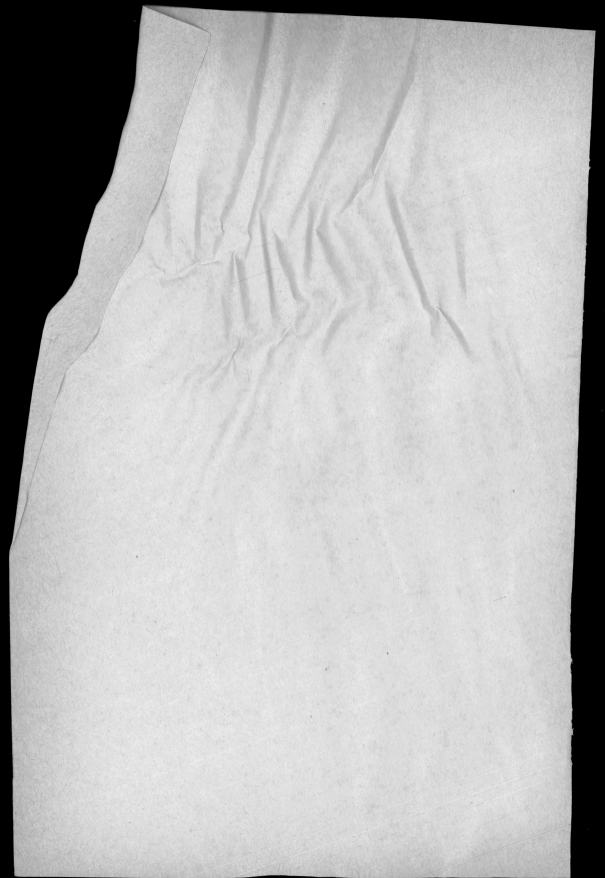